STAN TEKIELA's
Birding for
Beginners

California

Your Guide to Feeders, Food
and the Most Common Backyard Birds

by Stan Tekiela

Adventure Publications
Cambridge, Minnesota

DEDICATION

To the memory of my mother, Adele.

Edited by Brett Ortler and Dan Downing

Cover, book design and illustrations by Jonathan Norberg

Cover photos by Stan Tekiela. Front: House Finch **Back:** Downy Woodpecker
All photos by Stan Tekiela except pg. 78 by **Paul Bannick**; pg. 132 by **Albert Barr/Shutterstock**; pp. 92, 108, 172, 174 and 182 by **Rick and Nora Bowers**; pg. 20 (Barn Swallow) by **Mirko Graul/ Shutterstock**; pg. 102 by **Brian E. Kushner/Shutterstock**; pg. 20 (Northern Flicker) by **Anatoliy Lukich/ Shutterstock**; pg. 166 (female) by **Thomas Morris/Shutterstock**; pp. 74 (female) and 76 by **Sundry Photography/Shutterstock**; pg. 152 (displaying) by **Hartmut Walter**; pg. 160 (juvenile) by **Brian K. Wheeler**; and pg. 148 (brown morph) by **Jim Zipp**

To the best of the publisher's knowledge, all photos were of live birds. Some were photographed in a controlled condition.

10 9 8 7 6 5 4 3 2

Stan Tekiela's Birding for Beginners: California
First Edition 2020
Copyright © 2020 by Stan Tekiela
Published by Adventure Publications
An imprint of AdventureKEEN
310 Garfield Street South
Cambridge, Minnesota 55008
(800) 678-7006
www.adventurepublications.net
All rights reserved
Printed in the United States of America
ISBN 978-1-64755-112-4 (pbk.); ISBN 978-1-64755-113-1 (ebook)

Table of Contents

Getting Started

Welcome to the world of birding! If you're a beginner trying to identify the birds in your backyard, this book is for you. Birding is a simple pastime that's incredibly popular, and it's not hard to see why: You can watch birds in any season, and as far as hobbies go, a basic setup is about as cheap as it gets. All you need is some green space, a bird feeder and perhaps a pair of binoculars. I've written this book to help birders who are just starting out. This book contains 63 species of birds in California, all common visitors to backyards and bird feeders. It includes favorites such as orioles, bluebirds and hummingbirds and familiar visitors such as quails, chickadees and nuthatches.

Once you start identifying backyard birds, I'd encourage you to find my state-specific field guide for California. It contains 170 species of birds, including a wide variety of birds you're not as likely to see in your average backyard, including raptors, shorebirds and more. It also contains a detailed range map for each species, showing when and where each bird is usually found.

I sincerely hope you enjoy your start to bird watching. Have fun, and again, welcome!

Black-chinned Hummingbird male

Bird Feeder Basics

To get more birds to visit your yard, an easy way to invite them is to put out bird feeders. Bird feeders are often as unique as the birds themselves, so the types of feeders you use really depends on the kinds of birds you're trying to attract.

Hopper feeders are often wooden or plastic. Designed to hold a large amount of seeds, they often have a slender opening along the bottom, which dispenses the seeds. Birds land along the sides and help themselves to the food. Hopper feeders work well as main feeders in conjunction with other types of feeders. They are perfect for offering several kinds of seed mixes for grosbeaks, finches, nuthatches, chickadees and more.

Tube feeders with large seed ports and multiple perches are very popular. Often mostly plastic, they tend to be rugged enough to last several years and can be easily cleaned. These feeders are great for black oil sunflower seeds and seed mixes, which are favorites of grosbeaks and all the other bird species that also visit hopper feeders.

Some tube feeders have small holes, allowing incredibly tiny thistle seeds to be dispensed just a few at a time. Use this kind of feeder to offer Nyjer seed, which will attract various finches.

Other styles of tube feeders have a wire mesh covering with openings large enough for birds to extract one of their favorite foods—peanuts out of the shell. Most birds enjoy peanuts, so these feeders will be some of the most popular in your yard. Another variety of tube feeder has openings large enough for peanuts in the shell. These are also very popular with the birds.

Ground feeders allow a wide variety of birds to access the food. The simplest and easiest feeders to use, they consist of a flat platform with a lip around the edges to keep seeds from spilling out. Some have a roof to keep rain and snow off the food. With or without a roof, drainage holes in the bottom are important. Ground feeders will bring in juncos and many other birds to your backyard, including mallards if you're near water.

Suet feeders are simply wire cages that hold cakes of suet. The wire allows woodpeckers, nuthatches and other birds to cling securely to the feeder while pecking out chunks of suet. The best suet feeders have a vertical extension at the bottom where a woodpecker can brace its tail and support itself while feeding. These are called tail-prop suet feeders.

Nectar feeders are glass or plastic containers that hold sugar water. These feeders usually have plastic parts that are bright red, a color that is extremely attractive to hummingbirds, but orioles and woodpeckers will also stop for a drink. They often have up to four ports for access to the liquid and yellow bee guards to prevent bees from getting inside.

Mealworm feeders can be very basic—a simple glass or plastic cup or container will do. Pick one with sides tall enough and make sure the material is slippery enough to stop the lively mealworms from crawling out. Bluebirds especially love this wiggly treat!

Get to Know Your Birdseed

 **Black Oil Sunflower:** Studies have shown that all birds prefer black oil sunflower seeds over all other commercial bird foods. Black oilers are smooth black seeds that come from the common sunflower plant, *Helianthus annuus*. Even smaller birds such as finches have no trouble cracking open these seeds with their large, strong bills.

Black oilers contain more fat in the form of oil than other seeds, hence the name. They are meatier and pack more nourishment per bite than just about any other bird food on the market. Each seed has a nutritional value of 28% fat, 15% protein and 25% fiber and supplies vitamins B and E as well as calcium, iron and potassium.

 **Striped Sunflower:** Striped sunflower seeds have a thin white stripe. They are larger than black oilers, and they have a thicker hull, making them harder to split. Nevertheless, Steller's Jays open them easily and like them immensely. Occasionally called stripers, these are the sunflower seeds that people eat. High in fat, protein, vitamins and fiber, they are usually a part of any popular birdseed mix.

 **White Safflower:** This is a good option for those who want to avoid attracting squirrels and grackles, which often find it distasteful and difficult to open. It attracts many backyard favorites, such as grosbeaks, chickadees and more. Smaller than black oil seed, safflower is a thick-shelled, small white seed that is high in nutrition and fat. These seeds come from the annual safflower plant, *Carthamus tinctorius*.

Golden Safflower: Enjoyed by nuthatches, chickadees and other strong-billed birds, this is an improved variety of white safflower that is also called NutraSaff safflower. Introduced in 2004, it has a thinner outer hull, high oil content, high protein and polyunsaturated omega-6 fatty acids. Developed as food for beef and dairy cattle, poultry and fish and for bird feed markets.

Hulled Sunflower: Hulled sunflower is just the meat (or nutmeat) of the sunflower seed without the hard, inedible outer shell. The nutritional content is the same as black oil and striped sunflower seeds. There is no possibility for these seeds to germinate, so the bags are marketed as "non-germinating" or "no-mess" mixes. With hulled sunflower, you won't need to rake up or blow away discarded hulls under your feeders.

Hulled sunflower is often available as whole nuts or as pieces or chips. The expense of shelling the seeds makes this feed more expensive than others, but the benefits may outweigh the cost. After all, most birdseed is sold by weight, and with hulled sunflower you are not paying for the inedible shells.

White Millet: Millet is a soft-shelled, small round grain that comes from the millet plant, *Panicum milieaceum*. There are red, golden and striped varieties of millet, but the most common for bird feeding is proso millet, which is white.

White millet attracts a variety of birds, including sparrows, juncos and doves. It contains good nutritional content: around 4% fat, 12% protein and 8% fiber, vitamin B and calcium. An affordable seed that is usually offered in ground and tray feeders, it is also sprinkled on the ground to attract birds to the feeders.

 **Cracked Corn:** At a wonderful low cost, cracked corn is a great option to feed large numbers of wild birds on the ground. It also attracts rabbits, squirrels, raccoons and opossums. Offerings of cracked corn will keep the squirrels busy with something to eat, keeping them from your feeders filled with the higher-priced foods for the birds.

Cracked corn is exactly what it sounds like—dried whole corn kernels that have been cracked open. There can be a lot of dust associated with cracked corn, but it's worth it. This food won't sprout and grow in your garden or lawn, and birds/squirrels eat everything, so there's no waste. Low in fat but high in protein and fiber, it is often a base in bird food blends. Offer it in large open-tray, fly-through or ground feeders or sprinkle it around on the ground.

 **Whole Corn:** Whole corn consists of unbroken kernels of dried corn and is often part of the base of wild bird food mixes. It is less desirable to birds than cracked corn and usually is thought of as wildlife food since it attracts squirrels, chipmunks, raccoons, opossums and other animals. You can offer it in a large tray or trough ground feeder or spread it on the ground.

 **Peanuts:** Peanuts are another option to feed birds. The peanut plant, *Arachis hypogaea*, is a member of the legume or bean family and the peanuts grow underground. Peanuts contain about 45% fat and 24% protein, and they are a good source of vitamins A and E as well as zinc, iron and potassium.

Peanut pieces are popular in seed mixes and suet. Many birds will eat them in any form—shelled, in small chips or whole in the shell. They gobble up peanuts quickly, so sprinkle them with a feed mix or place them in a feeder with a tight mesh to prevent large amounts from spilling out all at once.

You can also try offering peanuts in the shell to birds. Put them in a larger mesh feeder with large openings so the birds can extract the entire nut. Peanuts get wet and tend to mold, so avoid putting out a lot at one time.

MIXES

Songbird Mix: Just about every major retailer has its own version of a songbird mix. It is often a combination of black oil sunflower seeds, striped sunflower seeds, safflower, cracked corn and other ingredients. The amount and proportion of seeds vary from store to store, but the main seed in these mixes are black oil seeds. To start getting familiar songbirds to come to your yard, offer a songbird mix.

Premium or Deluxe Blend: Premium blends are often a base of black oil sunflower seeds combined with striped sunflower seeds and safflower. The addition of peanuts, shelled or whole, upgrades any regular blend to premium or deluxe. Sometimes these mixtures also contain raisins, cranberries or other dried fruit. All sorts of birds love this rich food, and it is great for winter when you want to offer an extra-special treat.

Non-germinating Mix: Non-germinating mixes are composed of seeds that have been removed from their shells. Because seeds without shells will not germinate, people who don't want rogue sunflowers growing in their lawns or gardens may want to try it.

These mixes often have 2–3 varieties of seeds, with whole nuts or pieces of seed meat. Non-germinating may look like the most expensive seed per pound, but you're not paying for hulls, which are included in the weight of other seeds but aren't eaten.

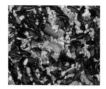

Specialty Mix: Many seed stores make a specialty blend that is unique to their store and works well for their region. In California, black oil sunflower seed is the main ingredient. Stores may also mix more striped sunflower seeds, safflower, peanuts or cracked or whole corn with seeds.

Other Foods

Suet: Another way to attract birds, especially woodpeckers, is to offer suet. Suet cakes are composed mainly of beef fat. Specifically, it is cow fat from around the kidneys and loins. However, more and more suet is coming from cow fat anywhere on the animal.

Suet is an extremely high-energy food with a high calorie count, and many birds can easily digest it. Some varieties are mixed with seeds, nuts or dried fruit. Suet in these forms is a great way to give your backyard birds an especially tasty treat.

Offer suet in specialized wire feeders with a bottom perch. These allow birds to reach in to the cake and break off small pieces. Hang your suet feeders in areas where squirrels, chipmunks, raccoons and opossums will have trouble accessing them, otherwise, they will take the entire cake.

 **Mealworms:** Mealworms are the worm-like larvae of darkling beetles, which are flightless insects. An excellent source of protein, calcium and vitamins, the offering of mealworms will attract bluebirds, as well as a variety of birds that don't normally come to traditional seed feeders.

Mealworms can be purchased live or dried. Both are sold in large quantities, and for good reason. When birds find them, they gorge themselves. Live mealworms must be stored in a container from which they cannot escape. A steep container with slippery sides is essential, and it should be refrigerated. Offer dried mealworms in a shallow tray.

 **Fresh & Dried Fruit:** Offering fresh fruit, such as orange halves, is a popular way to bring in orioles and other popular birds. Many fresh fruits, including bananas, apples, melons and grapes, and dried fruits, such as raisins, currants and prunes, are good choices to put out.

Orioles will come to orange halves placed sunny-side up and impaled on a nail to secure them. Fresh fruit slices can become messy and attract insects and mammals. To keep animals away, provide the fruit on a platform with a squirrel or raccoon baffle.

Grape Jelly: Orioles and other birds also like the sweet taste of grape jelly. They will come to this highly sugared, high-energy food early in spring when the weather can be cold and wet. Many types of commercial jelly feeders are available, but you can offer the treat in a small tray, cup or other container. To prevent the birds from getting jelly on their feathers, offer small portions each time.

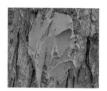

Peanut Butter: Regular smooth or chunky peanut butter is another good food to attract a wide variety of birds to your yard. Offer it like suet in specialized feeders or just smear it on a chunk of bark, directly onto a tree or on a suet cake. You can offer this high-energy food in your own creative ways. However you present it, birds will quickly find it.

Storing Birdseed and Feeder Maintenance

Storing birdseed safely is easy. Keep it out of the house, preferably in a cool, dry place away from direct sunlight. Garages and sheds are the best places to stow feed since the cooler temperatures there will reduce the number of grain moths hatching out of the seeds.

Transfer seed out of its original plastic or paper bag into a clean container. The container should be upright, semi-airtight and prevent mice, chipmunks and other rodents from chewing through and getting to the seed. Metal garbage cans are good choices for storage. Use several to store different kinds of food.

Try to avoid buying bird food in very large quantities. Pick up just enough to feed birds for a month or so. Make sure you use up the oldest seed before opening your more recent purchases.

Always try to use rubber gloves when handling your feeders and cleaning the feeding area because there are several diseases that can be picked up from bird droppings. Histoplasmosis is a disease caused by breathing in *Histoplasma capsulatum*, a fungus in soils that comes from bird and bat droppings. It is recommended to wear a particulate mask while raking up or blowing away seed hulls underneath feeders. Many people who contract histoplasmosis don't develop symptoms, but some exhibit mild flu-like symptoms and, rarely, serious complications.

Cryptococcosis is another fungal disease found in the environment, and it also comes from bird droppings. Often associated with pigeon droppings, it is best to wear rubber gloves and a mask when cleaning up scat on feeders and around roosting sites, attics, cupolas and other places where large numbers of birds gather. Like histoplasmosis, many people don't suffer any symptoms, and some come down with mild flu-like symptoms.

West Nile virus is carried by mosquitoes. Crows, jays and other birds contract it but don't transfer it to humans, so there is no need to be concerned about getting this disease from your feeders.

Keeping your feeding station clean and refreshing the site are quick and easy ways to stop the spread of avian disease and other diseases from bird droppings.

What's That Bird? Tips for Identifying Birds

Identifying birds isn't as difficult as you might think. By simply following a few basic strategies, you can increase your chances of successfully identifying most birds that you see. One of the first and easiest things to do when you see a new bird is to note its **color**. This field guide is organized by color, so simply turn to the right color section to find it.

House Sparrow   American Robin   American Crow   Canada Goose

Next, note the **size of the bird.** A strategy to quickly estimate size is to compare different birds. Pick a small, a medium and a large bird. Select an American Robin as the medium bird. Measured from bill tip to tail tip, a robin is 10 inches (25 cm). Now select two other birds, one smaller and one larger. Good choices are a House Sparrow, at about 6 inches (15 cm), and an American Crow, around 18 inches (45 cm). When you see a species you don't know, you can now quickly ask yourself, "Is it larger than a sparrow but smaller than a robin?" When you look in your field guide to identify your bird, you would check the species that are roughly 6–10 inches (15–25 cm). This will help to narrow your choices.

Rufous
Hummingbird   House Finch   Hairy Woodpecker   Cooper's Hawk

Next, note the **size, shape and color of the bill.** Is it long or short, thick or thin, pointed or blunt, curved or straight? Seed-eating birds, such as finches, have bills that are thick and strong enough to crack even the toughest seeds. Birds that sip nectar, such as Anna's Hummingbirds, need long, thin bills to reach deep into flowers. Hawks and owls tear their prey with very sharp, curving bills. Sometimes, just noting the bill shape can help you decide whether the bird is a woodpecker, finch, grosbeak, blackbird or bird of prey.

Northern Flicker

Noticing **what the bird is eating** will give you another clue to help you identify the species. Feeding is a big part of any bird's life. Fully one-third of all bird activity revolves around searching for food, catching prey and eating. While birds don't always follow all the rules of their diet, you can make some general assumptions.

Northern Flickers, for instance, feed on ants and other insects, so you wouldn't expect to see them visiting a seed feeder. Other birds, such as Barn and Tree Swallows, eat flying insects and spend hours swooping and diving to catch a meal.

Barn Swallow

Birds in flight are harder to identify, but noting the **wing size and shape** will help. Wing size is in direct proportion to body size, weight and type of flight. Wing shape determines whether the bird flies fast and with precision, or slowly and less precisely. Barn Swallows, for instance, have short, pointed wings that slice through the air, enabling swift, accurate flight. House Finches have short, rounded wings, helping them to flit through thick tangles of branches.

Some bird species have a unique **pattern of flight** that can help in identification. Pileated Woodpeckers fly in a distinctive undulating pattern (next page) that makes it look like they're riding a roller coaster.

While it's not easy to make all of these observations in the short time you often have to watch a "mystery" bird, practicing these identification methods will greatly expand your birding skills. To further improve your skills, seek the guidance of a more experienced birder who can answer your questions on the spot.

Bird Basics

It's easier to identify birds and communicate about them if you know the names of the different parts of a bird. For instance, it's more effective to use the word "crest" to indicate the set of extra-long feathers on top of a Northern Cardinal's head than to try to describe it. The following illustration points out the basic parts of a bird. Because it is a composite of many birds, it shouldn't be confused with any actual bird.

House Finch: male, female

BIRD COLOR VARIABLES

No other animal has a color palette like birds. Brilliant blues, lemon yellows, showy reds and iridescent greens are common in the bird world. In general, male birds are more colorful than their female counterparts. This helps males attract a mate, essentially saying, "Hey, look at me!" Color calls attention to a male's health as well. The better the condition of his feathers, the better his food source, territory and potential for mating.

When male and female birds of the same species don't look like each other, they are called sexually dimorphic, meaning "two forms." Dimorphic females often have a nondescript, dull color, as seen in House Finches. Muted tones not only help females hide during the weeks of motionless incubation but also draw less attention to them when they're out feeding or taking a break from the rigors of raising the young.

The males and females of some species, such as the Downy Wood-pecker, Steller's Jay and Bald Eagle, look nearly identical. In woodpeckers, they are differentiated by only a red (sometimes yellow or black) mark; this mark may be on top of the head, on the face or nape, or just behind the bill.

During the first year, juvenile birds often look like their mothers. Since brightly colored feathers are used mainly for attracting a mate, young non-breeding males don't have a need for colorful plumage. It's not until the first spring molt (or several years later, depending on the species) that young males obtain their breeding colors.

Both breeding and winter plumages are the result of molting. Molting is the process of dropping old, worn feathers and replacing them with new ones. All birds molt, typically twice a year, with the spring molt usually occurring in late winter. At this time, most birds produce their brighter breeding plumage, which lasts throughout the summer.

American Goldfinch winter plumage

Winter plumage is the result of the late-summer molt, which serves a couple of important functions. First, it adds feathers for warmth in the coming winter season. Second, in some species it produces feathers that tend to be drab in color, which helps to camouflage the birds and hide them from predators. The winter plumage of the male American Goldfinch, for example, is olive brown, unlike its canary-yellow breeding color during summer. Luckily for us, some birds, such as the male Blue Grosbeak, retain their bright summer colors all year long.

BIRD NESTS

Bird nests are a true feat of engineering. Imagine constructing a home that's strong enough to weather storms, large enough to hold your entire family, insulated enough to shelter them from cold and

American Goldfinch

heat, and waterproof enough to keep out rain. Think about building it without blueprints or directions and using mainly your feet. Birds do this!

Before building, birds must select an appropriate site. In some species, such as the House Wren, the male picks out several potential sites and assembles small twigs in each. The "extra" nests, called dummy nests, discourage other birds from using any nearby cavities for their nests. The male takes the female around and shows her the choices. After choosing her favorite, she finishes the construction.

In other species, such as the Baltimore Oriole, the female selects the site and builds the nest, while the male offers an occasional suggestion. Each bird species has its own nest-building routine that is strictly followed.

As you can see in the photos on pp. 25–27, birds build a wide variety of nests.

Nesting material often consists of natural items found in the immediate area. Most nests consist of plant fibers (such as bark from grapevines), sticks, mud, dried grass, feathers, fur or soft, fuzzy tufts from thistle. Some birds, including Ruby-throated Hummingbirds, use spiderwebs to glue nest materials together.

Transportation of nesting material is limited to the amount a bird can hold or carry. Birds must make many trips afield to gather enough material to complete a nest. Most nests take four days or more, and hundreds, if not thousands, of trips to build.

Canada Goose nest

A **ground nest** can be a mound of vegetation on the ground or in the water. It can also be just a simple, shallow depression scraped out in earth, stones or sand. Killdeer and Horned Larks scrape out ground nests without adding any nesting material.

Double-crested Cormorant nest

The **platform nest** represents a much more complex type of construction. Typically built with twigs or sticks and branches, this nest forms a platform and has a depression in the center to nestle the eggs. Platform nests can be in trees; on balconies, cliffs, bridges or man-made platforms; and even in flowerpots. They often provide space for the adventurous young and function as a landing platform for the parents.

Mourning Doves and herons don't anchor their platform nests to trees, so these can tumble from branches during high winds and storms. Hawks, eagles, ospreys and other birds construct sturdier platform nests with large sticks and branches.

Other platform nests are constructed on the ground with mud, grass and other vegetation from the area. Many waterfowl build platform nests on the ground near or in water. A **floating platform nest** moves with the water level, preventing the nest, eggs and birds from being flooded.

Northern Cardinal nest

Three-quarters of all songbirds construct a **cup nest,** which is a modified platform nest. The supporting platform is built first and attached firmly to a tree, shrub or rock ledge, or it is built on the ground. Next, the sides are constructed with grass, small twigs, bark or leaves, which are woven together and often glued with mud for added strength. The inner cup is contoured last and can be lined with down feathers, animal fur or hair, or soft plant materials.

The **pendulous nest** is an unusual nest that looks like a sock hanging from a branch. Attached to the end of small branches of trees, this unique nest is inaccessible to most predators and often waves wildly in a breeze.

Baltimore Oriole nest

Woven tightly with plant fibers, the pendulous nest is strong and watertight and takes up to a week to build. A small opening at the top or on the side allows parents access to the grass-lined interior. More commonly used by tropical birds, this complex nest has also been mastered by orioles and kinglets. It must be one heck of a ride to be inside one of these nests during a windy spring thunderstorm!

The **cavity nest** is used by many species of birds, most notably woodpeckers and Mountain and Western Bluebirds. A cavity nest is often excavated from a branch or tree trunk and offers shelter from storms, sun, cold and predators. A small entrance hole in a tree can lead to a nest chamber that is up to a safe 10 inches (25 cm) deep.

Red-bellied Woodpecker nest

Typically made by woodpeckers, cavity nests are usually used only once by the builder. Nest cavities can be used for many subsequent years by inhabitants such as Tree Swallows, mergansers and bluebirds. Kingfishers, on the other hand, can dig a tunnel up to 4 feet (1 m) long into a riverbank. The nest chamber at the end of the tunnel is already well insulated, so it's usually only sparsely lined.

Indigo Bunting nest with Brown-headed Cowbird egg (speckled)

One of the most clever of all nests is the **no nest,** or daycare nest. Parasitic birds, such as Brown-headed Cowbirds, don't build their own nests. Instead, the egg-laden female searches out the nest of another bird and sneaks in to lay an egg while the host mother isn't looking.

A mother cowbird wastes no energy building a nest only to have it raided by a predator. Laying her eggs in the nests of other birds transfers the responsibility of raising her young to the host. When she lays her eggs in several nests, the chances increase that at least one of her babies will live to maturity.

WHO BUILDS THE NEST?

Generally, the female bird constructs the nest. She gathers the materials and does the building, with an occasional visit from her mate to check on progress. In some species, both parents contribute equally. The male may forage for sticks, grass or mud, but the female often fashions the nest. Only rarely does a male build a nest by himself.

WHY BIRDS MIGRATE

Why do so many species of birds migrate? The short answer is simple: food. Birds migrate to locations with abundant food, as it is easier to breed where there is food than where food is scarce. Scarlet Tanagers, for instance, are **complete migrators** that fly from the tropics of South America to nest in the forests of North America, where billions of newly hatched insects are available to feed to their young.

Other migrators, such as some birds of prey, migrate back to northern regions in spring. In these locations, they hunt mice, voles and other small rodents that are beginning to breed.

Complete migrators have a set time and pattern of migration. Every year at nearly the same time, they head to a specific wintering ground.

Pacific / Central / Mississippi / Atlantic

Major migratory flyways

Complete migrators may travel great distances, sometimes 15,000 miles (24,100 km) or more in one year.

Complete migration doesn't necessarily mean flying from Ohio to a tropical destination. Some Dark-eyed Juncos, for example, live in California year-round, while others migrate here from northern U.S. states or the far reaches of Canada. This trip is still considered complete migration.

Complete migrators have many interesting aspects. In spring, males often leave a few weeks before the females, arriving early to scope

Dark-eyed Junco female

out possibilities for nesting sites and food sources and to begin to defend territories. The females arrive several weeks later. In many species, the females and their young leave earlier in the fall, often up to four weeks before the adult males.

Other species, such as the Anna's Hummingbird, are **partial migrators.** These birds usually wait until their food supplies dwindle before flying south. Unlike complete migrators, partial migrators move only far enough south, or sometimes east and west, to find abundant food. In some years it might be only a few hundred miles, while in other years it can be as many as a

Anna's Hummingbird male

thousand. This kind of migration, dependent on weather and the availability of food, is sometimes called seasonal movement.

Unlike the predictable complete migrators or partial migrators, **irruptive migrators** may move every third to fifth year or, in some cases, in consecutive years. These migrations are triggered when times are tough and food is scarce. Red-breasted Nuthatches are irruptive migrators. They leave their normal northern range in search of more food or in response to overpopulation.

Many other birds don't migrate at all. American Crows, for example, are **non-migrators** that remain in their habitat all year long and only move around as necessary to find food.

Tips for a Bird-Friendly Yard

Plant native plants—a green lawn looks pretty, but it doesn't offer all that much for birds or other wildlife. A yard full of native or other flowering plants, on the other hand, is like putting out the welcome mat for birds, especially when those plants offer cover (think shrubs/bushes), food sources (native and non-native cultivated plants, wildflowers or fruit-bearing trees) or nesting materials or sites. And you don't need a huge space to help the birds: Even a container garden with native plants can help!

Avoid insecticides, herbicides and other chemical treatments. Many birds depend on insects as a major part of their diet, and the same is true of weed seeds. Most insecticides on the market are broad-spectrum, which means they kill the bugs you're targeting (mosquitoes!) but many other insects that too, including bees, butterflies and the like.

Provide bird food consistently, along with water. Consistency is key when it comes to bird feeding. If you only happen to put out birdseed once in a while, you'll attract fewer birds than if you do so regularly. Choose high-quality birdseed, and offer a variety of foods, if possible. When you're putting out bird food, provide a birdbath too. Don't feed birds if your feeder potentially puts birds in danger (e.g., where a window strike could happen or near a busy road).

Downy Woodpecker

Keep cats indoors. Cats are a major threat to birds and other wildlife. If you have a house cat, keep it indoors.

Do-it-Yourself Bird Food

A BASIC PEANUT BUTTER SPREAD FOR BIRDS

Ingredients:
½ cup raisins
½ cup granola
½ cup oatmeal
½ cup Cheerios
16-ounce jar smooth peanut butter

Directions: Mix dry ingredients in a large mixing bowl. Warm the peanut butter in a microwave or place the jar in warm water to soften. Scoop out the softened peanut butter, and mix it well with the dry ingredients until smooth.

Spread on tree bark or smear a few dollops on the tray of a feeder.

A SIMPLE SUET RECIPE

Ingredients:
2 cups suet or lard
1 cup peanut butter
2 cups yellow cornmeal
2 cups cracked corn
1 cup black oil sunflower seeds

Directions: In a large pot, melt the suet or lard over low heat. Add the peanut butter, stirring until melted and well mixed. Add remaining ingredients, and mix.

Pour into baking pans or forms and allow to cool. Cut into chunks or shapes. Store in freezer.

Birding Citizen Science

RARE BIRD SIGHTINGS

To report unusual bird sightings or possibly hear recordings of where birds have been seen, you can often call prerecorded hotlines detailing such information. Since these hotlines are usually staffed by volunteers, and phone numbers and even the organizations that host them often change, the phone numbers are not listed here. To obtain the numbers, go to your favorite internet search engine, type in something like "rare bird alert hotline California" and follow the links provided.

BIRD COUNTS AND CITIZEN SCIENCE

Bird watching isn't just a fun pastime; your observations can actually help science. With habitat fragmentation and climate change harming bird populations, it's essential for biologists to have accurate, up-to-date population totals for birds, especially those that are potentially threatened or endangered.

But tracking birds is tricky; that's where two long-running bird-tracking programs—and you—come in. Think of each as a census for the birds. One is **The Christmas Bird Count,** which has been around for 120 years. Held from mid-December to early January, volunteers spread out to count birds in specific areas around each state and the country, with counts occurring in a local area for only one day. (So if you want to join in on the fun, prepare ahead of time!)

California Quail male

The **Great Backyard Bird Count** is similar, but it takes place everywhere, and you can participate if you bird for as little as 15 minutes, making it easy to join. It takes place in February.

Frequently Asked Questions

Why aren't birds showing up to my feeders? It's exciting to put up your bird feeders, but you can't always expect birds to show up right away. It takes time for birds to find feeders, so patience is key. Do your best to feed consistently, offer a variety of foods and offer a water source.

What do I do if there's a bird I can't recognize or find in this book?
In California, birders have sighted hundreds of different species of birds. This book focuses on common backyard birds; for that reason, most shorebirds, raptors and the like are not included. Once you bird beyond the backyard, check out *Birds of California*, with 170 species of birds. See page 190.

House Finch male

Should I put out a birdbath? What about mosquitoes? Yes! Putting out a birdbath is a great way to attract birds; to prevent mosquito larvae from taking up residence there, purchase a "water wiggler." These devices agitate the water, preventing it from being suitable for mosquitoes. (Plus, the sound of the moving water attracts birds on its own.)

Help! There are squirrels at my feeders. This is an age-old problem. There are a number of possible solutions, from squirrel baffles and greased bird feeder poles, to buying birdseed treated with hot peppers, which squirrels don't like. On the other hand, there are also feeders specifically for squirrels, including more than a few that are quite inventive.

I found an egg/nest/feather. Can I keep it? Disturbing birds, their nests and even keeping their feathers is against the law in nearly all cases. The reason is simple: Many bird species almost went extinct due to unchecked hunting, egg collection and the use of feathers for high-end fashion. Today, migratory birds are protected by federal law. Instead, take some photos of your find and use the internet to attempt to identify it.

I found a baby bird, or an adult bird that is injured. What should I do? If you find a baby bird, chances are its parent is nearby; in most cases, you simply need to leave it be. If you see an injured bird, you can contact your local wildlife rehabilitation facility and follow their instructions/advice.

American Robin

How to Use This Guide

To help you quickly and easily identify birds, this field guide is organized by color. It also only features birds that are commonly seen in average backyards or at bird feeders.

Refer to the color key on the first page, note the color of the bird and then turn to that section. For example, the Spotted Towhee is black-and-white with red sides. Because the bird is mostly black, it will be found in the black section.

Each color section is also arranged by size, generally with the smaller birds first. Descriptions may indicate the average size as a range, which in some cases reflects size differences between male and female birds. Flip through the pages in the color section to find the bird. If you already know the name of the bird, check the checklist/index for the page number.

Look for field marks called out to make identification easier

male

female
pg. 103

Common Name
Scientific name

Size: measurement is from head to tip of tail; may include the wingspan

Male: brief description of the male bird; may include breeding, winter or other plumages

Female: brief description of the female bird, which is sometimes different from the male

Juvenile: brief description of the juvenile bird, which often looks like the adult female

Nest: kind of nest the bird builds to raise its young; who builds it; number of broods per year

Eggs: number of eggs you might expect to see in a nest; color and marking

When Seen: the approximate season(s) when you're likely to see the bird; some birds are seen year-round

Food: what the bird eats most of the time (e.g., seeds, insects, fruit, nectar, small mammals, fish); if it typically comes to a bird feeding station

Compare: notes about other birds that look similar and the pages on which they can be found; may include extra information to aid identification

Stan's Notes: Interesting gee-whiz natural history information. This could be something to look or listen for, or something to help positively identify the bird. Also includes remarkable features.

Look for the brown head

male

female
pg. 105

Brown-headed Cowbird

Molothrus ater

Size: 7½" (19 cm)

Male: A glossy black bird with a chocolate-brown head and pointed, sharp gray bill. Dark eyes.

Female: dull brown with a pointed gray bill

Juvenile: similar to female, but dull gray plumage with a streaked chest

Nest: no nest; lays eggs in the nests of other birds

Eggs: 5–7; white with brown markings

When Seen: year-round along coast, spring and summer

Food: insects, seeds; will come to seed feeders

Compare: Male Red-winged Blackbird (pg. 45) is slightly larger and has red-and-yellow patches on its upper wings. European Starling (pg. 41) has a shorter tail.

Stan's Notes: Cowbirds are members of the blackbird family. Known as brood parasites, Brown-headed Cowbirds are the only parasitic birds in California. Brood parasites lay their eggs in the nests of other birds, leaving the host birds to raise their young. Cowbirds are known to have laid their eggs in the nests of over 200 species of birds. While some birds reject cowbird eggs, most incubate them and raise the young, even to the exclusion of their own. Look for warblers and other birds feeding young birds twice their own size. Named "Cowbird" for its habit of following bison and cattle herds to feed on insects flushed up by the animals.

Look for the iridescent feathers

breeding

winter

European Starling

Sturnus vulgaris

Size: 7½" (19 cm)

Male: Glittering, iridescent purplish-black in spring and summer, duller and speckled with white in fall and winter. Long, pointed yellow bill in spring, gray in fall. Pointed wings. Short tail.

Female: same as male

Juvenile: similar to adult, with grayish-brown plumage and a streaked chest

Nest: cavity; male and female line cavity; 2 broods per year

Eggs: 4–6; bluish with brown markings

When Seen: year-round

Food: insects, seeds, fruit; visits seed or suet feeders

Compare: Male Brown-headed Cowbird (pg. 39) has a brown head. Look for the shiny dark feathers to help identify the European Starling.

Stan's Notes: One of our most numerous songbirds. Mimics the songs of up to 20 bird species and imitates sounds, including the human voice. Jaws are more powerful when opening rather than closing, enabling the bird to pry open crevices to find insects. Often displaces woodpeckers, chickadees and other cavity-nesting birds. Large families gather with blackbirds in the fall. Not a native bird; 100 starlings were introduced to New York City in 1890–91 from Europe. Bill changes color with the seasons in spring and fall.

*Look for the
ragged crest*

male

female
pg. 147

Phainopepla

Phainopepla nitens

Size: 8" (20 cm)

Male: Slim, long, glossy black bird with a ragged crest and deep red eyes. Wing patches near tips of wings are white, obvious in flight.

Female: slim, long, mostly gray bird with a ragged crest and deep red eyes, whitish wing bars

Juvenile: similar to female

Nest: cup; female and male construct; 1–2 broods per year

Eggs: 2–4; gray with brown markings

When Seen: year-round

Food: fruit (usually mistletoe), insects; will come to water elements or water drips in yards

Compare: The only all-black bird with a crest and red eyes. Look for white wing patches in flight.

Stan's Notes: Seen in desert scrub with water and mistletoe nearby. Gives a low, liquid "kweer" song, but will also mimic other species. In winter individuals defend food supply such as a single tree with abundant mistletoe berries. Probably responsible for the dispersal of mistletoe plants far and wide. Male will fly up to a height of 300 feet (90 m), circling and zigzagging to court female. Builds nest of twigs and plant fibers and binds it with spider webs in the crotch of a mistletoe cluster. Lines nest with hair or soft plant fibers. May be the only species to nest in two regions in the same nest season. Nests in dry desert habitat in early spring. When it gets hot, moves to a higher area with an abundant water supply to nest again.

*Look for the
red-and-yellow
shoulder patches*

male

female
pg. 111

Red-winged Blackbird
Agelaius phoeniceus

Size:	8½" (21.5 cm)
Male:	Jet-black with red-and-yellow patches on the upper wings (epaulets). Pointed black bill.
Female:	heavily streaked brown bird with a pointed brown bill and white eyebrows
Juvenile:	same as female
Nest:	cup; female builds; 2–3 broods per year
Eggs:	3–4; bluish-green with brown markings
When Seen:	year-round
Food:	seeds, insects; visits seed and suet feeders
Compare:	The male Brown-headed Cowbird (pg. 39) is smaller, glossier and has a brown head. The bold red-and-yellow epaulets distinguish the male Red-winged from all other blackbirds.

Stan's Notes: One of the most widespread and numerous birds in California. Found around marshes, wetlands, lakes and rivers. Flocks with as many as 10,000 birds have been reported. Males arrive before the females and sing to defend their territory. The male repeats his call from the top of a cattail while showing off his red-and-yellow shoulder patches. The female chooses a mate and often builds her nest over shallow water in a thick stand of cattails. The male can be aggressive when defending the nest. Feeds mostly on seeds in spring and fall, and insects throughout the summer.

Look for the dirty red-brown sides

male

female

Spotted Towhee
Pipilo maculatus

Size: 8½" (22 cm)

Male: Mostly black with dirty red-brown sides and a white belly. Multiple white spots on wings and sides. Long black tail with a white tip. Rich, red eyes.

Female: very similar to male but with a brown head

Juvenile: brown with a heavily streaked chest

Nest: cup; female builds; 1–2 broods per year

Eggs: 3–5; white with brown markings

When Seen: year-round

Food: seeds, fruit, insects

Compare: Closely related to the Green-tailed Towhee (pg. 169), which lacks the bold black and red colors. Smaller than American Robin (pg. 151).

Stan's Notes: Found in a variety of habitats, from thick brush and chaparral to suburban backyards. Usually heard noisily scratching through dead leaves on the ground for food. Over 70 percent of its diet is plant material. Eats more insects during spring and summer. Well known to retreat from danger by walking away rather than taking to flight. Nest is nearly always on the ground under bushes but away from where the male perches to sing. Begins breeding in April. Lays eggs in May. After the breeding season, moves to higher elevations. Song and plumage vary geographically and aren't well studied or understood.

*Look for the
exceptionally long tail*

female
pg. 119

Great-tailed Grackle

Quiscalus mexicanus

Size: 18" (45 cm), male
15" (38 cm), female

Male: Large all-black bird with iridescent purple sheen on the head and back. Exceptionally long tail. Bright-yellow eyes.

Female: considerably smaller than the male, overall brown bird with gray-to-brown belly, light-brown-to-white eyes, eyebrows, throat and upper chest

Juvenile: similar to female

Nest: cup; female builds; 1–2 broods per year

Eggs: 3–5; greenish blue with brown markings

When Seen: year-round

Food: insects, fruit, seeds; comes to seed feeders

Compare: Male Brown-headed Cowbird (pg. 39) lacks the Great-tailed Grackle's long tail and has a brown head.

Stan's Notes: This is our largest grackle. It was once considered a subspecies of the Boat-tailed Grackle which occurs along the East Coast and Florida. A colony nester. Males do not participate in nest building, incubation or raising young. Males rarely fight; females squabble over nest sites and materials. Several females mate with one male. Western populations tend to be larger than eastern. Song varies from population to population.

Look for the glossy black feathers

in flight

American Crow

Corvus brachyrhynchos

Size: 18" (45 cm)

Male: All-black bird with a black bill, legs and feet. Can have a purple sheen in direct sunlight.

Female: same as male

Juvenile: same as adult

Nest: platform; female builds; 1 brood per year

Eggs: 4–6; bluish-to-olive with brown markings

When Seen: year-round

Food: fruit, insects, mammals, fish, carrion; comes to seed and suet feeders

Compare: Similar to the Common Raven (pg. 53) but the American Crow has a smaller bill, lacks shaggy throat feathers and has a higher-pitched call than the Raven's deep, low raspy call. The American Crow has a squared tail. The Raven has a wedge-shaped tail, apparent in flight.

Stan's Notes: A familiar bird, found in all habitats. Imitates other birds and human voices. One of the smartest of all birds and very social, often entertaining itself by provoking chases with other birds. Eats roadkill but rarely hit by vehicles. Can live up to 20 years. Often reuses its nest every year if not taken over by a Great Horned Owl. Unmated birds, known as helpers, help to raise the young. Extended families roost together at night, dispersing daily to hunt. Cannot soar on thermals. Flaps constantly and glides downward. Gathers in huge communal flocks of up to 10,000 birds in winter.

Look for the
shaggy feathers
on throat and chin

in flight

Common Raven

Corvus corax

Size: 22–27" (56–69 cm)

Male: Large all-black bird with a shaggy beard of feathers on throat and chin. Large black bill. Large wedge-shaped tail, best seen in flight.

Female: same as male

Juvenile: same as adult

Nest: platform; female and male construct; 1 brood per year

Eggs: 4–6; pale green with brown markings

When Seen: year-round

Food: insects, fruit, small animals, carrion

Compare: American Crow (pg. 51) is smaller and lacks the shaggy throat feathers. Glides on flat, outstretched wings unlike the slightly V-shaped pattern of the Crow. Low raspy call, compared with the higher-pitched call of the Crow.

Stan's Notes: Considered by some people to be the smartest of all birds. Known for its aerial acrobatics and long swooping dives. Soars on wind without flapping, like a raptor. Sometimes scavenges with crows and gulls. A cooperative hunter that often communicates the location of a good source of food to other ravens. Most start to breed at 3–4 years. Complex courtship includes grabbing bills, preening each other and cooing. Long-term pair bond. Uses the same nest site for many years.

Look for the small, short bill

male

female

Downy Woodpecker

Dryobates pubescens

Size: 6" (15 cm)

Male: A small woodpecker with a white belly and black-and-white spotted wings. Red mark on the back of head and a white stripe down the back. Short black bill.

Female: same as male, but lacks a red mark on head

Juvenile: same as female, some have a red mark near the forehead

Nest: cavity with a round entrance hole; male and female excavate; 1 brood per year

Eggs: 3-5; white without markings

When Seen: year-round

Food: insects, seeds; visits suet and seed feeders

Compare: Hairy Woodpecker (pg. 61) is larger. Look for the shorter, thinner bill to identify the Downy.

Stan's Notes: Abundant and widespread where trees are present. This is perhaps the most common woodpecker in the U.S. Stiff tail feathers help to brace it like a tripod as it clings to a tree. Like other woodpeckers, it has a long, barbed tongue to pull insects from tiny places. Mates drum on branches or hollow logs to announce territory, which is rarely larger than 5 acres (2 ha). Repeats a high-pitched "peek-peek" call. Nest cavity is wider at the bottom than at the top and is lined with fallen woodchips. Male performs most of the brooding. During winter, it will roost in a cavity. Undulates in flight.

*Look for the
white belly*

Black Phoebe

Sayornis nigricans

Size: 7" (18 cm)

Male: Black head, neck, breast and back with a white belly and undertail. Long narrow tail. Dark eyes, bill and legs. Can raise and lower its small crest.

Female: same as male

Juvenile: similar to adult, brown-to-tan wing bars

Nest: cup; female builds; 1–2 broods per year

Eggs: 3–6; white without markings

When Seen: year-round

Food: insects

Compare: The Black Phoebe's distinctive black-and-white pattern makes identification easy. Watch for the Black Phoebe to pump its tail up and down very quickly when perched.

Stan's Notes: Often seen in shrubby areas near water. Feeds mostly on insects near the surface of water. In the winter it feeds on insects near the ground. Like other flycatchers, perches on thin branches, flies out to snatch a passing insect and returns to perch. Pumps or bobs tail up and down quickly while perching. Male performs an aerial song and flight with a slow descent to attract a mate. Female builds shallow nest of mud, adhered to rocks or bridges, lined with hair and grass. Often uses same nest or location for several years.

Look for the red cap and nape

male

female

Nuttall's Woodpecker

Dryobates nuttallii

Size: 7½" (19 cm)

Male: Mostly black and white barred woodpecker with a red cap and nape. Dull white breast and belly with black spots. Two black lines, one through the eyes and another extending from the bill, connect behind the cheek.

Female: same as male, but lacks a red spot on head and nape

Juvenile: similar to male, red spot closer to forehead

Nest: cavity; male and female build; 1–2 broods per year

Eggs: 3–6; white without markings

When Seen: year-round

Food: insects, berries, seeds, tree sap

Compare: Downy (pg. 55) and Hairy (pg. 61) Woodpeckers have whiter breasts and bellies and a large white stripe on their backs.

Stan's Notes: A species unique to California. Prefers oak woodlands and moist areas with cottonwoods and willows. Creeps along a tree trunk, often boring a small hole to get to wood-boring insects. Diet consists of 80 percent insects. Pairs often stay together all year. Male defends territory. Usually excavates nest cavity in dead cottonwood, willow or alder tree near water. Nest is unlined. Male does the most incubating and brooding after the eggs hatch. Hybridization with Downy Woodpeckers often occurs where their ranges overlap.

Look for the large bill

male

female

Hairy Woodpecker

Dryobates villosus

Size: 9" (23 cm)

Male: A black-and-white woodpecker with a white belly. Black wings with rows of white spots. White stripe down the back. Long black bill. Red mark on the back of head.

Female: same as male, but lacks a red mark on head

Juvenile: grayer version of the female

Nest: cavity with an oval entrance hole; female and male excavate; 1 brood per year

Eggs: 3–6; white without markings

When Seen: year-round

Food: insects, nuts and seeds; will come to suet and seed feeders

Compare: The Hairy Woodpecker is much larger than Downy Woodpecker (pg. 55) and has a much longer bill, nearly equal to the width of its head. Nuttall's Woodpecker (pg. 59) lacks a large white stripe on its back.

Stan's Notes: A common bird in wooded backyards. Announces its arrival with a sharp chirp before landing on feeders. Responsible for eating many destructive forest insects. Uses its barbed tongue to extract insects from trees. Tiny bristle-like feathers at the base of the bill protect the nostrils from wood dust. Drums on hollow logs, branches or stovepipes in spring to announce territory. Often prefers to excavate nest cavities in live aspen trees. Excavates a larger, more oval-shaped entrance than the round entrance hole of the Downy Woodpecker. Makes short flights from tree to tree.

Look for the white eyes

male

female

Acorn Woodpecker

Melanerpes formicivorus

Size: 9" (22.5 cm)

Male: A black and white woodpecker with an all-black back and prominent white eyes. Red cap and nape of neck. White forehead and cheeks. White rump and tips of wings, seen in flight.

Female: same as male, but has a smaller bill and less red on head

Juvenile: similar to adult of the same sex

Nest: cavity; male and female excavate; 1 brood per year

Eggs: 3–7; white without markings

When Seen: year-round

Food: nuts, fruit, insects, sap; comes to suet and seed feeders

Compare: The Downy Woodpecker (pg. 55) and the Hairy Woodpecker (pg. 61) have white backs. Look for the white eye and black back of the Acorn Woodpecker.

Stan's Notes: A woodpecker that depends upon acorns and other nuts for survival. Dead trees are very important to this species, as they are to all woodpeckers. Drills uniform holes in trees and telephone poles, where it wedges acorns and other nuts, storing them for later consumption. Unlike other woodpeckers, it lives and nests in small colonies. Colonies consist of up to 5 males, 1–2 females and up to 12 juveniles from previous years. All members help to raise the new young. This is a very vocal species, giving a loud, nasal, "wheka-wheka-wheka" call.

Look for the white chin and chest

Tree Swallow

Tachycineta bicolor

Size: 5–6" (13–15 cm)

Male: Blue-green in spring, greener in fall. Changes color in direct sunlight. White from chin to belly. Long, pointed wing tips. Notched tail.

Female: similar to male, only duller

Juvenile: gray-brown with a white belly and a grayish breast band

Nest: cavity; female and male line a vacant woodpecker cavity or nest box; 2 broods per year

Eggs: 4–6; white without markings

When Seen: year-round

Food: insects

Compare: The Barn Swallow (pg. 69) has a rusty belly and a long, deeply forked tail. Look for the white chin, chest and belly and the notched tail to identify the Tree Swallow.

Stan's Notes: Found at ponds, lakes, rivers and farm fields. Often seen flying back and forth across fields, feeding on insects. Can be attracted to your yard with a nest box. Competes with bluebirds for tree cavities and nest boxes. Builds a grass nest within and will travel long distances, looking for dropped feathers for the lining. Watch for it playing, chasing after feathers. Flies with rapid wingbeats, then glides. Gives a series of gurgles and chirps. Chatters when upset or threatened. Eats many nuisance bugs, so it's good to have around. Families gather in large flocks for migration.

Look for the turquoise blue head

male

female
pg. 93

Lazuli Bunting

Passerina amoena

Size: 5½" (14 cm)

Male: A turquoise blue head, neck, back and tail. Cinnamon chest with cinnamon extending down flanks slightly. White belly. Two bold white wing bars. Non-breeding male has a spotty blue head and back.

Female: overall grayish brown, warm brown breast, a light wash of blue on wings and tail, gray throat, light gray belly and 2 narrow white wing bars

Juvenile: similar to adult of the same sex

Nest: cup; female builds; 2–3 broods per year

Eggs: 3–5; pale blue without markings

When Seen: summer

Food: insects, seeds

Compare: The male Western Bluebird (pg. 75) is larger and darker blue with a darker brown breast. The male Blue Grosbeak (pg. 71) has chestnut wing bars and lacks a white belly.

Stan's Notes: More common in shrub lands in California. Doesn't like dense forests. Strong association with water such as rivers and streams. Gathers in small flocks and tends to move up in elevations after breeding to hunt for insects and look for seeds. Has increased in population and expanded its range over the last century.

Look for the deeply forked tail

Barn Swallow

Hirundo rustica

Size: 7" (18 cm)

Male: A sleek swallow. Blue-black back, cinnamon belly and reddish-brown chin. White spots on a long, deeply forked tail.

Female: same as male, but has a whitish belly

Juvenile: similar to adults, with a tan belly and chin and a shorter tail

Nest: cup; female and male build; 2 broods per year

Eggs: 4–5; white with brown markings

When Seen: summer

Food: insects (prefers beetles, wasps, flies)

Compare: Tree Swallow (pg. 65) is white from chin to belly. Look for the deeply forked tail to help identify the Barn Swallow.

Stan's Notes: Seen in wetlands, farms, suburban yards and parks. California has seven swallow species, but this is the only one with a deeply forked tail. Unlike other swallows, it rarely glides in flight. Usually flies low over land or water. Drinks as it flies, skimming water, or will sip water droplets on wet leaves. Bathes while flying through rain or sprinklers. Gives a twittering warble, followed by a mechanical sound. Builds a mud nest with up to 1,000 beak-loads of mud. Nests on barns, houses, under bridges and other sheltered places. Often nests in colonies of 4–6 birds; sometimes nests alone.

Look for the two chestnut wing bars

male

female
pg. 103

Blue Grosbeak

Passerina caerulea

Size:	7" (18 cm)
Male:	Overall blue bird with 2 chestnut wing bars. Large gray-to-silver bill. Black around base of bill.
Female:	overall brown with darker wings and tail, 2 tan wing bars, large gray-to-silver bill
Juvenile:	similar to female
Nest:	cup; female builds; 1–2 broods per year
Eggs:	3–6; pale blue without markings
When Seen:	summer
Food:	insects, seeds; will come to seed feeders
Compare:	The male Lazuli Bunting (pg. 67) has 2 bold white wing bars and a white belly. The male Mountain and Western Bluebirds (pp. 73 and 75, respectively) are the same size, but lack the male Grosbeak's chestnut wing bars and oversized bill.

Stan's Notes: This grosbeak returns to California in early May. A bird of semi-open habitats such as overgrown fields, riversides, woodland edges and fencerows. Visits seed feeders. Frequently seen twitching and spreading its tail. The first-year males show only some blue, obtaining the full complement of blue feathers in the second winter. It has expanded northward, and its overall populations have increased over the past 30–40 years.

male

Look for the
overall blue

Look for the
gray head

female

Mountain Bluebird

Sialia currucoides

Size: 7" (18 cm)

Male: Overall sky-blue bird with a darker blue head, back, wings and tail. White lower belly. Thin black bill.

Female: similar to male, but paler with a nearly gray head and chest and a whitish belly

Juvenile: similar to adult of the same sex

Nest: cavity, old woodpecker cavity, wooden nest box; female builds; 1–2 broods per year

Eggs: 4–6; pale blue without markings

When Seen: year-round

Food: insects, fruit

Compare: Western Bluebird (pg. 75) is similar, but is darker blue with a rusty-red chest. Male Blue Grosbeak (pg. 71) is the same size, but it has chestnut wing bars and a large bill.

Stan's Notes: The Mountain Bluebird is common in mountainous country. Its main diet is insects, and it often hovers before diving to the ground to grab an insect. Due to conservation of suitable nesting sites (dead trees with cavities and man-made nest boxes), populations have increased over the past 30 years. Like other bluebirds, Mountain Bluebirds take well to nest boxes and tolerate close contact with people. The female sits on baby birds (brood) for up to six days after the eggs hatch. The young imprint on their first nest box or cavity and choose a similar nest box or cavity later in life. Look for Mountain Bluebirds in any open field.

male

*Look for
the rusty red chest
and flanks*

*Look for
the gray head*

female

Western Bluebird
Sialia mexicana

Size: 7" (18 cm)

Male: Deep blue head, neck, throat, back, wings and tail. Rusty red chest and flanks.

Female: similar to male, only duller with a gray head

Juvenile: similar to female, with a speckled chest

Nest: cavity, old woodpecker cavity, wooden nest box; female builds; 1–2 broods per year

Eggs: 4–6; pale blue without markings

When Seen: year-round

Food: insects, fruit

Compare: Mountain Bluebird (pg. 73) is similar but lacks the rusty-red breast. Larger than male Lazuli Bunting (pg. 67), which has white wing bars. Male Blue Grosbeak (pg. 71) is the same size but has chestnut wing bars and an oversized bill.

Stan's Notes: Found in a variety of habitats, from agricultural land to clear-cuts. Requires a cavity for nesting. Competes with starlings for nest cavities. Like the Mountain Bluebird, it uses nest boxes, which are responsible for the stable populations. Populations dropped during the mid-1900s but recovered due to the efforts of concerned people who put up nest boxes, providing much-needed habitats for nesting. A courting male will fly in front of the female, spread his wings and tail, and perch next to her. Often goes in and out of its nest box or cavity as if to say, "Look inside." Male may offer food to the female to establish a pair bond.

*Look for the
brownish patch
on back*

California Scrub-Jay

Aphelocoma californica

Size:	11" (28 cm)
Male:	A bird with a deep blue head, wings, tail, and breast band. Brownish patch on back. Chin, breast and belly are dull white. Very long tail.
Female:	same as male
Juvenile:	similar to adult, overall gray with light blue wings and tail
Nest:	cup; female and male build; 1 brood a year
Eggs:	3–6; pale green with red brown markings
When Seen:	year-round
Food:	insects, seeds, fruit; comes to seed feeders
Compare:	Same size as Steller's Jay (pg. 79), but lacks the all-black head and pointed crest.

Stan's Notes: A tame bird of urban areas that visits feeders. Forms a long-term pair bond. The male feeds the female before and during incubation. Young of a pair remain close by for up to a couple years, helping parents raise subsequent siblings. Caches food by burying it for later consumption. The California Scrub-Jay likely helps distribute oak and pine trees as it doesn't eat all of the seeds it buries.

Look for the black head and crest

Steller's Jay
Cyanocitta stelleri

Size: 11" (28 cm)

Male: A striking bird with dark blue wings, tail, and belly. Black head, nape and breast. Large, pointed black crest on head that can be lifted at will.

Female: same as male

Juvenile: similar to adult

Nest: cup; female and male build; 1 brood a year

Eggs: 3–5; pale green with brown markings

When Seen: year-round

Food: insects, berries, seeds; will visit seed feeders

Compare: The California Scrub-Jay (pg. 77) lacks the Steller's crest and all-black head.

Stan's Notes: Common resident of coniferous forests from sea level to timberline. Often found in suburban yards. Thought to mate for life, rarely dispersing far, usually breeding within 10 miles (16 km) of birthplace. Several subspecies found throughout the Southwest. The California form (shown) has a black crest and lacks any distinct white streaks on head. Usually very bold where it comes in contact with people on a regular basis such as a campground. Often seen in small flocks consisting mainly of family members. Feeds on a wide variety of foods, but seeds make up 70 percent of the diet. Will cache seeds and acorns for later consumption. Was named after the Arctic explorer Georg W. Steller, the first European to record the bird. He sighted it on the coast of Alaska in 1741.

Look for the rusty crown

Chipping Sparrow
Spizella passerina

Size: 5" (13 cm)

Male: Small gray-brown sparrow with a clear gray chest, white eyebrows, thin black eye line and rusty crown. Thin gray-black bill. Two faint wing bars.

Female: same as male

Juvenile: similar to adult, with streaking on the chest; lacks a rusty crown

Nest: cup; female builds; 2 broods per year

Eggs: 3–5; blue-green with brown markings

When Seen: spring through fall

Food: insects, seeds; will come to ground feeders

Compare: The Song Sparrow (pg. 89), Fox Sparrow (pg. 101) and female House Finch (pg. 85) have heavily streaked chests. Look for the rusty crown and black eye line to identify the Chipping Sparrow.

Stan's Notes: A common garden or yard bird, often seen feeding on dropped seeds beneath feeders. Gathers in large family groups to feed in preparation for migration. Migrates at night in flocks of 20–30 birds. The common name comes from the male's fast "chip" call. Often just called Chippy. Builds nest low in dense shrubs and almost always lines it with animal hair. Comfortable with people, allowing you to approach closely before it flies away.

Look for the yellow on the wings

Pine Siskin
Spinus pinus

Size: 5" (13 cm)

Male: Small brown finch with heavy streaking on the back, breast and belly. Yellow wing bars. Yellow at the base of tail. Thin bill.

Female: similar to male, with less yellow

Juvenile: similar to adult, with a light yellow tinge over the breast and chin

Nest: cup; female builds; 2 broods

Eggs: 3–4; greenish-blue with brown markings

When Seen: winter

Food: seeds, insects; will come to seed feeders

Compare: Female House Finch (pg. 85) lacks any yellow. Female American Goldfinch (pg. 181) has white wing bars. Look for the yellow wing bars to identify the Pine Siskin.

Stan's Notes: Usually considered a winter finch. Conspicuous in some winters, rare in others. Seen in flocks of up to 20 birds, often with other finch species. Gathers in flocks and moves around, visiting feeders. Will come to thistle feeders. Gives a series of high-pitched, wheezy calls. Also gives a wheezing twitter. Breeds in small groups. Builds nest toward the end of coniferous branches, where needles are dense, helping to conceal. Nests are often only a few feet apart. Male feeds the female during incubation. Juveniles lose the yellow tint by late summer of their first year.

male
pg. 177

female

Look for the
heavily streaked chest

House Finch

Haemorhous mexicanus

Size:	5" (13 cm)
Female:	Plain brown bird with heavy streaking on a white chest.
Male:	red-to-orange face, throat, chest and rump, brown cap, brown marking behind the eyes, streaked belly and wings
Juvenile:	similar to female
Nest:	cup, occasionally in a cavity, female builds; 2 broods per year
Eggs:	4–5; pale blue, lightly marked
When Seen:	year-round
Food:	seeds, fruit, leaf buds; visits seed feeders and feeders that offer grape jelly
Compare:	Pine Siskin (pg. 83) has yellow wing bars and a smaller bill. Female American Goldfinch (pg. 181) has a clear chest. Look for the heavily streaked chest to help identify the female House Finch.

Stan's Notes: Can be a common bird at your feeders. A very social bird, visiting feeders in small flocks. Likes to nest in hanging flower baskets. Male sings a loud, cheerful warbling song. Native to parts of California and the western U.S., it was introduced to Long Island, New York in the 1940s, and it is now found throughout the country. Suffers from a disease that causes the eyes to crust, resulting in blindness and death.

Look for the
slightly curved bill

House Wren

Troglodytes aedon

Size: 5" (13 cm)

Male: All-brown bird with lighter brown markings on the wings and tail. Slightly curved brown bill. Often holds tail upward.

Female: same as male

Juvenile: same as adult

Nest: cavity; female and male line just about any nest cavity; 2 broods per year

Eggs: 4–6; tan with brown markings

When Seen: year-round

Food: insects, spiders, snails

Compare: Bewick's Wren (pg. 95) is larger and has white eyebrows. The slightly curved bill and upward position of the tail differentiates the House Wren from sparrows. Look for the curved bill and upturned tail to help identify the House Wren.

Stan's Notes: A prolific songster. During the mating season, sings from dawn to dusk. Seen in brushy yards, parks, woodlands and along forest edges. Easily attracted to a nest box. In spring, the male chooses several prospective nesting cavities and places a few small twigs in each. The female inspects all of them and finishes constructing the nest in the cavity of her choice. She fills the cavity with short twigs and then lines a small depression at the back with pine needles and grass. She often has trouble fitting longer twigs through the entrance hole and tries many different directions and approaches until she is successful.

Look for the central dark spot on the chest

Song Sparrow
Melospiza melodia

Size: 5–6" (13–15 cm)

Male: A common brown sparrow with heavy dark streaks on the chest coalescing into a central dark spot.

Female: same as male

Juvenile: similar to adult, with a finely streaked chest; lacks a central dark spot

Nest: cup; female builds; 2 broods per year

Eggs: 3–4; blue to green with red-brown markings

When Seen: year-round

Food: insects, seeds; only rarely comes to ground feeders with seeds

Compare: Similar to other brown sparrows. Look for the heavily streaked chest with a central dark spot to help identify the Song Sparrow.

Stan's Notes: There are many subspecies of this bird, but the dark spot in the center of the chest appears in every variety. A constant songster, repeating its loud, clear song every few minutes. The song varies from region to region but has the same basic structure. Sings from thick shrubs to defend a small territory, beginning with three notes and finishing up with a trill. A ground feeder, look for it to "double-scratch" with both feet at the same time to expose seeds. When the female builds a new nest for a second brood, the male often takes over feeding the first brood. Unlike many other sparrow species, Song Sparrows rarely flock together. A common host of the Brown-headed Cowbird.

Look for the ivory-to-pink bill

male
pg. 139

female

Oregon female

Dark-eyed Junco
Junco hyemalis

Size: 5½" (14 cm)

Female: A plump, dark-eyed bird with a tan-to-brown chest, head and back. White belly. Ivory-to-pink bill. White outer tail feathers appear like a white V in flight.

Male: round bird with gray plumage

Juvenile: similar to female, with streaking on the breast and head

Nest: cup; female and male build; 2 broods per year

Eggs: 3–5; white with reddish-brown markings

When Seen: year-round

Food: seeds, insects; visits ground and seed feeders

Compare: Rarely confused with any other bird. Look for the ivory-to-pink bill and small flocks feeding under feeders to help identify the female Dark-eyed Junco.

Stan's Notes: Northern birds join resident birds during winter, swelling the population. Migrates from Canada and northern parts of Minnesota to areas farther south. Adheres to a rigid social hierarchy, with dominant birds chasing the less dominant birds. Look for the white outer tail feathers flashing in flight. Often seen in small flocks on the ground, where it uses its feet to simultaneously "double-scratch" to expose seeds and insects. Eats many weed seeds. Nests in a wide variety of wooded habitats. Several junco species have now been combined into one, simply called Dark-eyed Junco (see lower inset).

Look for the light wash of blue on wings and tail

female

male
pg. 67

Lazuli Bunting

Passerina amoena

Size: 5½" (14 cm)

Female: Grayish-brown bird overall with a warm brown chest, light wash of blue on wings and tail, gray throat and light gray belly. Two narrow white wing bars.

Male: turquoise blue head, neck, back and tail, cinnamon breast, white belly, 2 bold white wing bars

Juvenile: similar to adult of the same sex

Nest: cup; female builds; 2–3 broods per year

Eggs: 3–5; pale blue without markings

When Seen: summer

Food: insects, seeds

Compare: Female Blue Grosbeak (pg. 103) is similar, but is darker overall and has tan wing bars. The female Western Bluebird (pg. 75) and Mountain Bluebird (pg. 73) are larger and have much more blue than the female bunting.

Stan's Notes: More common in shrublands in California. Doesn't like dense forests. Strong association with water such as rivers and streams. Gathers in small flocks and tends to move up in elevations after breeding to hunt for insects and look for seeds. Has increased in population and expanded its range over the last century.

*Look for the
white chin
and eyebrows*

Bewick's Wren

Thryomanes bewickii

Size: 5½" (14 cm)

Male: Brown cap, back, wings and tail. Gray chest and belly. White chin and eyebrows. Long tail with white spots on edges is cocked and flits sideways. Pointed down-curved bill.

Female: same as male

Juvenile: similar to adult

Nest: cavity; female and male build nest in woodpecker hole or nest box; 2–3 broods a year

Eggs: 4–8; white with brown markings

When Seen: year-round

Food: insects, seeds

Compare: The House Wren (pg. 87) is slightly smaller and lacks the obvious white eyebrow marks and white spots on tail.

Stan's Notes: A common wren of backyards and gardens. Insects make up 97 percent of its diet, with plant seeds composing the rest. Competes with House Wrens for nesting cavities. Male will choose nesting cavities and start to build nests using small uniform-sized sticks. Female will make the final selection of a nest site and finish building. Begins breeding in March and April. Has 2–3 broods per year. Male feeds female while she incubates. Average size territory per pair is 5 acres (2 ha), which they defend all year long.

*Look for
the black
throat patch*

male

*Look for
the tan stripe
through the eye*

female

House Sparrow
Passer domesticus

Size: 6" (15 cm)

Male: Brown back with a gray belly and cap. Large black patch extending from the throat to the chest (bib). One white wing bar.

Female: slightly smaller than the male, light brown with light eyebrows; lacks a bib and white wing bar

Juvenile: similar to female

Nest: cavity; female and male build a domed cup nest within; 2–3 broods per year

Eggs: 4–6; white with brown markings

When Seen: year-round

Food: seeds, insects, fruit; comes to seed feeders

Compare: The Chipping Sparrow (pg. 81) has a rusty crown. Look for the black bib to identify the male House Sparrow and the clear breast to help identify the female.

Stan's Notes: One of the first birdsongs heard in cities in spring. A familiar city bird, nearly always in small flocks. Also found on farms. Introduced from Europe in 1850 to Central Park in New York. Now seen throughout North America. Related to Old World sparrows; not a relative of any sparrows in the U.S. An aggressive bird that will kill young birds in order to take over the nest cavity. Uses dried grass, small scraps of plastic, paper and other materials to build an oversized domed nest in the cavity.

Look for the
black-and-white striped crown

juvenile

White-crowned Sparrow
Zonotrichia leucophrys

Size: 6½–7½" (16.5–19 cm)

Male: Brown with a gray chest and black-and-white striped crown. Small, thin pink bill.

Female: same as male

Juvenile: similar to adult, with black-and-brown stripes on the head

Nest: cup; female builds; 2 broods per year

Eggs: 3–5; greenish to bluish to whitish, with red-brown markings

When Seen: year-round

Food: insects, seeds, berries; visits ground feeders

Compare: The Song Sparrow (pg. 89) has a streaked chest. Look for the striped crown to help identify the White-crowned Sparrow.

Stan's Notes: Often in groups of up to 20 birds during migration, when it can be seen visiting ground feeders and feeding beneath seed feeders. A ground feeder that will "double-scratch" backward with both feet simultaneously to find seeds. Prefers scrubby areas, woodland edges and open or grassy habitats. The males are prolific songsters, singing in late winter while migrating northward. Males arrive at the breeding grounds before the females and sing from perches to establish territory. Males take most of the responsibility to raise the young while females start a second brood. Only 9–12 days separate the broods.

Look for the rusty brown streaks on the chest

Fox Sparrow

Passerella iliaca

Size: 7" (18 cm)

Male: A plump, brown sparrow with a gray head, back and rump. White chest and belly with rusty brown streaks. Rusty tail and wings.

Female: same as male

Juvenile: same as adult

Nest: cup; female builds; 2 broods per year

Eggs: 2–4; pale green with reddish markings

When Seen: year-round

Food: seeds, insects; comes to ground feeders

Compare: The Spotted Towhee (pg. 47) is found in a similar habitat, but the male towhee has a black head.

Stan's Notes: One of the largest sparrows. Often alone or in small groups. Found in shrubby areas, open fields and backyards. Comes to ground feeders and seen underneath seed feeders during migration, searching for seeds and insects. Like a chicken, it will "double-scratch" with both feet at the same time to look for food. Gives a series of rich notes lasting 2–3 seconds, usually singing from a perch hidden in a shrub. The common name "Sparrow" comes from the Anglo-Saxon word *spearwa*, meaning "flutterer," and applies to any small bird. "Fox" refers to its rusty color. Appears in several color variations, depending on the part of the country.

Look for the large gray-to-silver bill

female

male
pg. 71

Blue Grosbeak

Passerina caerulea

Size: 7" (18 cm)

Female: Overall brown with darker wings and tail. Two tan wing bars. Large gray-to-silver bill.

Male: blue bird with 2 chestnut wing bars; large gray-to-silver bill; black around base of bill

Juvenile: similar to female

Nest: cup; female builds; 1–2 broods per year

Eggs: 3–6; pale blue without markings

When Seen: summer

Food: insects, seeds; will come to seed feeders

Compare: The female Lazuli Bunting (pg. 93) is similar, but has 2 narrow white wing bars and is lighter in color overall. Look for the female grosbeak's large gray-to-silver bill.

Stan's Notes: This grosbeak returns to California by early May. A bird of semi-open habitats such as overgrown fields, riversides, woodland edges and fencerows. Visits seed feeders. Often seen twitching and spreading its tail. The first-year males show only some blue, obtaining the full complement of blue feathers in the second winter. It has expanded northward, and its overall populations have increased over the past 30–40 years.

Look for the pointed gray bill

female

male
pg. 39

Brown-headed Cowbird

Molothrus ater

Size: 7½" (19 cm)

Female: Dull brown bird with no obvious markings. Pointed, sharp gray bill. Dark eyes.

Male: glossy black with a chocolate-brown head

Juvenile: similar to female, but dull gray plumage with a streaked chest

Nest: no nest; lays eggs in the nests of other birds

Eggs: 5–7; white with brown markings

When Seen: year-round along coast, spring and summer

Food: insects, seeds; will come to seed feeders

Compare: Female Red-winged Blackbird (pg. 111) has white eyebrows and heavy streaking. Look for the pointed gray bill to help identify the female Brown-headed Cowbird.

Stan's Notes: Cowbirds are members of the blackbird family. Known as brood parasites, Brown-headed Cowbirds are the only parasitic birds in California. Brood parasites lay their eggs in the nests of other birds, leaving the host birds to raise their young. Cowbirds are known to have laid their eggs in the nests of over 200 species of birds. While some birds reject cowbird eggs, most incubate them and raise the young, even to the exclusion of their own. Look for warblers and other birds feeding young birds twice their own size. Named "Cowbird" for its habit of following bison and cattle herds to feed on insects flushed up by the animals.

1 year old

Look for the
waxy-looking
red wing tips

Bohemian
Waxwing

Cedar Waxwing
Bombycilla cedrorum

Size: 7½" (19 cm)

Male: A sleek-looking gray-to-brown bird. Pointed crest, bandit-like mask and light yellow belly. Bold yellow tip of tail. Red wing tips look like they were dipped in red wax.

Female: same as male

Juvenile: grayish with a heavily streaked breast; lacks a sleek look, black mask and red wing tips

Nest: cup; female and male construct; 1 brood per year, occasionally 2

Eggs: 4–6; pale blue with brown markings

When Seen: winter

Food: cedar cones, fruit, seeds, insects

Compare: Bohemian Waxwing (see inset), is larger, less common and has white on its wings and rust under its tail. Look for the red wing tips to help identify the Cedar Waxwing.

Stan's Notes: The name is derived from its red wax-like wing tips and preference for the small, berry-like cones of the cedar. Seen in flocks, moving around from area to area, looking for berries. Feeds on insects during summer, before berries are abundant. Wanders during winter, searching for food supplies. Spends most of its time at the top of tall trees. Listen for the high-pitched "sreee" whistling sound it constantly makes while perched or in flight. Obtains the mask after the first year and red wing tips after the second year.

Look for the two-toned bill

female

male
pg. 173

Black-headed Grosbeak

Pheucticus melanocephalus

Size: 8" (20 cm)

Female: Appears like an overgrown sparrow. Overall brown with a lighter breast and belly. Large two-toned bill. Prominent white eyebrows. Yellow wing linings, as seen in flight.

Male: burnt-orange chest, neck and rump, black head, tail and wings with irregular-shaped white wing patches, large bill with upper bill darker than lower

Juvenile: similar to adult of the same sex

Nest: cup; female builds; 1 brood per year

Eggs: 3–4; pale green or bluish, brown markings

When Seen: summer

Food: seeds, insects, fruit; comes to seed feeders

Compare: Female House Finch (pg. 85) is smaller, has more streaking on the chest and the bill isn't as large. Look for female Grosbeak's unusual bicolored bill.

Stan's Notes: A cosmopolitan bird that nests in a wide variety of habitats. Both the male and female sing and will aggressively defend the nest against intruders. Song is very similar to American Robin's (pg. 151), making it hard to tell them apart by song. Populations increasing in California and across the U.S.

Look for the white eyebrows

female

male pg. 45

Red-winged Blackbird

Agelaius phoeniceus

Size: 8½" (21.5 cm)

Female: Heavily streaked brown bird with a pointed brown bill and white eyebrows.

Male: jet-black bird with red-and-yellow shoulder patches (epaulets) and a pointed black bill

Juvenile: same as female

Nest: cup; female builds; 2–3 broods per year

Eggs: 3–4; bluish-green with brown markings

When Seen: year-round

Food: seeds, insects; visits seed and suet feeders

Compare: Female Brown-headed Cowbird (pg. 105) lacks any streaks or white eyebrows and is slightly smaller. Look for white eyebrows and heavy streaking to identify the female Red-winged.

Stan's Notes: One of the most widespread and numerous birds in California. Found around marshes, wetlands, lakes and rivers. Flocks with as many as 10,000 birds have been reported. Males arrive before the females and sing to defend their territory. The male repeats his call from the top of a cattail while showing off his red-and-yellow shoulder patches. The female chooses a mate and often builds her nest over shallow water in a thick stand of cattails. The male can be aggressive when defending the nest. Feeds mostly on seeds in spring and fall, and insects throughout the summer.

*Look for the
two black neck bands*

Killdeer
Charadrius vociferus

Size: 11" (28 cm)

Male: An upland shorebird with two black bands around the neck, like a necklace. Brown back and white belly. Bright reddish-orange rump, visible in flight.

Female: same as male

Juvenile: similar to adult, with a single neck band

Nest: ground; male scrapes; 2 broods per year

Eggs: 3–5; tan with brown markings

When Seen: year-round

Food: insects; also worms, snails

Compare: By virtue of its habitat, there's not a lot you can confuse with the Killdeer.

Stan's Notes: Technically classified as a shorebird but lives in dry habitats instead of the shore. Often found in vacant fields, gravel pits, driveways, wetland edges or along railroad tracks. The only shorebird that has two black neck bands. Known to fake a broken wing to draw intruders away from the nest. Once the nest is safe, the parent will take flight. Nests are just a slight depression in a dry area and are often hard to see. Hatchlings look like miniature adults walking on stilts. Soon after hatching, the young follow their parents around and peck for insects. Gives a loud and distinctive "kill-deer" call. Migrates in small flocks.

Look for the red mustache

male

female

Northern Flicker

Colaptes auratus

Size: 12" (30 cm)

Male: Brown-and-black bird with a red mustache and black necklace. Speckled chest. Gray head with a brown cap. Large white rump patch, seen only when flying.

Female: same as male, but lacks a red mustache

Juvenile: same as adult of the same sex

Nest: cavity; female and male excavate; 1 brood per year

Eggs: 5–8; white without markings

When Seen: year-round

Food: insects (especially ants and beetles); comes to suet feeders

Compare: Nuttall's Woodpecker (pg. 59) is smaller and has a red cap and nape and lacks the Flicker's red mustache. Look for the gray-to-brown head to identify the Flicker.

Stan's Notes: This is the only woodpecker to regularly feed on the ground. Prefers ants and beetles and produces an antacid saliva that neutralizes the acidic defense of ants. The male often picks the nest site. Parents take up to 12 days to excavate the cavity. Can be attracted to your yard with a nest box stuffed with sawdust. Often reuses an old nest. Undulates deeply during flight, flashing reddish orange under its wings and tail, and calling "wacka-wacka" loudly.

Look for the
small head

Mourning Dove
Zenaida macroura

Size: 12" (30 cm)

Male: Smooth, fawn-colored dove. Gray patch on the head. Iridescent pink and greenish-blue on neck. Single black spot behind and below eyes. Black spots on wings and tail. Pointed, wedged tail with white edges, seen in flight.

Female: similar to male, but lacks the pink-and-green iridescent neck feathers

Juvenile: spotted and streaked plumage

Nest: platform; female and male build; 2 broods per year

Eggs: 2; white without markings

When Seen: year-round

Food: seeds; will visit ground and seed feeders

Compare: Lacks the wide range of color combinations of the Rock Pigeon (pg. 159).

Stan's Notes: Name comes from its mournful cooing. A ground feeder, bobbing its head as it walks. One of the few birds to drink without lifting its head, same as the Rock Pigeon. Parents feed the young (squab) a regurgitated liquid called crop-milk during their first few days of life. Platform nest is so flimsy that it often falls apart in a storm. During takeoff and in flight, wind rushes through its wing feathers, creating a characteristic whistling sound.

Look for the white eyes

female

male
pg. 49

Great-tailed Grackle

Quiscalus mexicanus

Size: 15" (38 cm), female
18" (45 cm), male

Female: An overall brown bird with a gray-to-brown belly.
Light-brown-to-white eyes, eyebrows, throat and
upper portion of chest.

Male: all-black bird with iridescent purple sheen on head and
back, exceptionally long tail, bright-yellow eyes

Juvenile: similar to female

Nest: cup; female builds; 1–2 broods per year

Eggs: 3–5; greenish blue with brown markings

When Seen: year-round

Food: insects, fruit, seeds; comes to seed feeders

Compare: The Great-tailed female is much larger than the female
Brown-headed Cowbird (pg. 105).

Stan's Notes: This is our largest grackle. It was once considered a sub-species of the Boat-tailed Grackle, which occurs along the East Coast and Florida. Prefers to nest close to water in an open habitat. A colony nester. Males do not participate in nest building, incubation or raising young. Males rarely fight; females squabble over nest sites and materials. Several females mate with one male. Western populations tend to be larger than eastern. Song varies from population to population.

Look for the feather tufts on the head

Great Horned Owl

Bubo virginianus

Size: 21–25" (53–64 cm); up to 4' wingspan

Male: A robust brown "horned" owl. Bright yellow eyes and V-shaped white throat, resembling a necklace. Horizontal barring on the chest.

Female: same as male, only slightly larger

Juvenile: similar to adults, but lacks ear tufts

Nest: no nest; takes over the nest of a crow or hawk, or uses a partial cavity, stump or broken tree; 1 brood per year

Eggs: 2–3; white without markings

When Seen: year-round

Food: mammals, birds (ducks), snakes, insects

Compare: Over twice the size of its cousin, Western Screech-Owl (pg. 149). Look for bright yellow eyes and feather "horns" on the head to help identify the Great Horned Owl.

Stan's Notes: One of the earliest nesting birds in California, laying eggs in January and February. Can hear a mouse move beneath a leaf pile or a foot of snow. "Ears" are tufts of feathers (horns) and have nothing to do with hearing. Cannot turn its head all the way around. Wing feathers are ragged on the ends, resulting in silent flight. Eyelids close from the top down, like ours. Fearless, it is one of the few animals that will kill skunks and porcupines. Given that, it is also called Flying Tiger. Call sounds like "hoo-hoo-hoo-hoooo."

Look for the overall brown and white streaking

displaying

Greater Roadrunner
Geococcyx californianus

Size: 23" (58 cm)

Male: Overall brown with white streaking. Long, pointed brown bill. Extremely long tail. Blue patch just behind eyes. Short round wings are darker brown than body. Long gray legs with large feet. Has a conspicuous crest that can be raised and lowered.

Female: same as male

Juvenile: similar to adult

Nest: platform, low in a tree, shrub or cactus; the female and male build; 1–2 broods per year

Eggs: 4–6; white without markings

When Seen: year-round

Food: insects, reptiles, small mammals and birds

Compare: This ground dweller has a unique shape, an extremely long tail, and a prominent crest. It's hard to confuse with any other bird.

Stan's Notes: Ground dweller with a very long tail and prominent crest when raised. Cuckoo family member known to run quickly across the ground to catch prey. Crest is very prominent when raised. A formidable predator, able to run up to 15 miles (24 km) per hour. Flies short distances, usually in a low glide after a running takeoff. Raises its tail high, lowers it slowly. A slow, descending, low-pitched "coo-coo-coo-coo." Male does most incubating and feeding of young. Performs a distraction display to protect the nest. Young can catch prey four weeks after leaving the nest.

displaying male

Look for the bare blue-and-red head

female

non-displaying male

Wild Turkey

Meleagris gallopavo

Size: 36–48" (91–122 cm)

Male: A large brown-and-bronze bird with a naked blue-and-red head. Long, straight black beard in the center of chest. Tail spreads open like a fan. Spurs on legs.

Female: thinner and less striking than the male; often lacks a breast beard

Juvenile: same as adult of the same sex

Nest: ground; female builds; 1 brood per year

Eggs: 10–12; buff-white with dull brown markings

When Seen: year-round

Food: insects, seeds, fruit

Compare: This bird is quite distinctive and unlikely to be confused with any other.

Stan's Notes: The largest game bird in California, and the species from which the domestic turkey was bred. A strong flier that can approach 60 mph (97 kph). Can fly straight up, then away. Eyesight is three times better than ours. Hearing is also excellent; can hear competing males up to a mile away. Male has a "harem" of up to 20 females. Female scrapes out a shallow depression for nesting and pads it with soft leaves. Males are known as toms, females are hens, young are poults. Roosts in trees at night. It was eliminated from many states due to market hunting and loss of habitat by 1900. Not native to California, a subspecies of the eastern wild turkey from Texas was introduced to the state, from 1950s to the 1990s. Now doing very well.

Look for the gray-brown crown

Pygmy Nuthatch
Sitta pygmaea

Size: 4¼" (10.5 cm)

Male: Tiny gray-blue black bird with gray-brown crown. Creamy chest with a lighter chin. A relatively short tail, large head and long bill.

Female: same as male

Juvenile: same as adult

Nest: cavity; female and male construct; 1 brood per year

Eggs: 4–8; white with brown markings

When Seen: year-round

Food: insects, berries, seeds; will visit seed feeders

Compare: Smaller than the Red-breasted Nuthatch (pg. 131) and the White-breasted Nuthatch (pg. 135). The Pgymy has a cream-colored breast, but the Red-breasted's is a rusty red. The White-breasted has a distinctive black cap and a white chest. Look for the Pygmy's gray-brown head.

Stan's Notes: A nuthatch of pine forests. Unlike the White-breasted Nuthatch, the Pygmy Nuthatch requires mature pines with old or decaying wood. Usually drills its own nest cavity. While it does not migrate, it forms winter flocks with chickadees and other birds and moves around to find food. Usually feeds in the crown of a tree or at the ends of twigs and branches, where it searches for insects and seeds. This is unlike White-breasted and Red-breasted Nuthatches, which usually search trunks of trees for food.

Look for the tiny black bill

Bushtit
Psaltriparus minimus

Size: 4½" (11 cm)

Male: A dull gray bird with a slightly brown cap. Relatively long tail. Black eyes and legs, and a tiny black bill.

Female: same as male, but has pale yellow eyes

Juvenile: similar to adults, with dark brown eyes

Nest: pendulous; female and male construct; 1–2 broods per year

Eggs: 5–7; white without markings

When Seen: year-round

Food: insects, seeds, fruit; comes to seed feeders

Compare: The Mountain Chickadee (pg. 141) is larger and has a black crown and white on its face. The Oak Titmouse (pg. 143) has a crest. Look for the Bushtit's tiny black bill.

Stan's Notes: A lively bird, often seen in extended family flocks of up to 20 individuals in open woods and low woodlands. It is often seen with other bird species such as kinglets, wrens and chickadees. Easily picked out by its small size, long tail and the extremely short bill. Groups will roost together, huddling tightly to keep warm and save energy. Eyes are pale yellow in adult females, dark brown in juveniles and black in adult males. Away from the coast, adults lack the brown cap, appearing all dull gray.

male

Look for the
rusty-red chest

female

Red-breasted Nuthatch

Sitta canadensis

Size: 4½" (11 cm)

Male: Gray-backed bird with an obvious black eye line and black cap. Rust-red breast and belly.

Female: duller than the male and has a gray cap and pale undersides

Juvenile: same as female

Nest: cavity; male and female excavate a cavity or move into a vacant hole; 1 brood per year

Eggs: 5–6; white with red-brown markings

When Seen: winter, year-round in some regions

Food: insects, insect eggs, seeds; comes to seed and suet feeders

Compare: Slightly larger than the Pygmy Nuthatch (pg. 127) and smaller than White-breasted Nuthatch (pg. 135). Look for the rust-red breast and black eye line to help identify the Red-breasted Nuthatch.

Stan's Notes: The nuthatch climbs down trunks of trees headfirst, searching for insects. Like a chickadee, it grabs a seed from a feeder and flies off to crack it open. Wedges the seed into a crevice and pounds it open with several sharp blows. The name "Nuthatch" comes from the Middle English moniker *nuthak,* referring to the habit of hacking seeds open. Look for it in mature conifers, where it extracts seeds from pine cones. Excavates a cavity or takes an old woodpecker hole or a natural cavity and builds a nest. Gives a series of nasal "yank-yank-yank" calls.

juvenile

*Look for the
lemon-yellow
head*

male

female

Verdin

Auriparus flaviceps

Size: 4½" (11 cm)

Male: Light gray to silvery overall. Lemon-yellow head. Rusty-red shoulder patch, frequently hidden. Short, pointed dark bill. Dark mark between bill and eyes. Dark legs and feet.

Female: duller than male

Juvenile: overall gray, lacks the yellow head, dark bill and rusty-red shoulder patch

Nest: covered cup; male builds; 1–2 broods a year

Eggs: 4–5; bluish green with brown markings

When Seen: year-round

Food: seeds, insects, fruit, nectar; comes to nectar feeders and orange halves

Compare: Smaller than the Oak Titmouse (pg. 143), which as a crest and lacks a yellow head. The Mountain Chickadee (pg. 141) has an obvious black cap, chin and eye line.

Stan's Notes: A very friendly bird that can be a regular visitor to nectar feeders and orange halves. Often hides its rusty-red shoulder marks, confusing the novice bird watcher. Most easily identified as a tiny gray bird with a yellow head. Male builds several ball-shaped, conspicuous nests of thorny twigs, interweaves them with leaves and grass and lines them with feathers and plant down. Male shows the nest possibilities to female and she selects one. After fledging, young return to nest at night unlike most small birds, which leave and don't return for shelter. Often uses nest for several seasons.

male

Look for the white chest

female

White-breasted Nuthatch

Sitta carolinensis

Size: 5–6" (13–15 cm)

Male: Slate-gray with a white face, breast and belly, and a large white patch on the rump. Black cap and nape of neck. Bill is long and thin, slightly upturned. Chestnut undertail.

Female: similar to male, but has a gray cap and nape

Juvenile: similar to female

Nest: cavity; female and male build a nest within; 1 brood per year

Eggs: 5–7; white with brown markings

When Seen: year-round

Food: insects, insect eggs, seeds; comes to seed and suet feeders

Compare: Red-breasted Nuthatch (pg. 131) is smaller and has a rust-red belly and distinctive black eye line. Pygmy Nuthatch (pg. 127) lacks a black cap. Look for the white breast to help identify the White-breasted Nuthatch.

Stan's Notes: The nuthatch hops headfirst down trees, looking for insects that birds climbing up miss. Its climbing agility is due to an extra-long hind toe claw, or nail, that is nearly twice the size of its front claws. "Nuthatch," from the Middle English *nuthak,* refers to the bird's habit of wedging a seed in a crevice and hacking it open. Often seen in flocks with chickadees and Downy Woodpeckers. Mates stay together year-round, defending a small territory. Gives a characteristic "whi-whi-whi-whi" spring call during February and March.

Look for the yellow patches on the head, flanks and rump

male

first winter

female

Yellow-rumped Warbler

Setophaga coronata

Size: 5–6" (13–15 cm)

Male: Slate gray with black streaking on the chest. Yellow patches on the head, flanks and rump. White chin and belly. Two white wing bars.

Female: duller gray than the male, mixed with brown

Juvenile: first winter is similar to the adult female

Nest: cup; female builds; 2 broods per year

Eggs: 4–5; white with brown markings

When Seen: winter, year-round in some regions, summer in others

Food: insects, berries; visits suet feeders in spring

Compare: Male White-breasted Nuthatch (pg. 135) is similar in size and color to male Yellow-rumped, but it lacks yellow patches on the head, flanks and rump. Female Lesser Goldfinch (pg. 179) is similar to female Yellow-rumped, but it is dull yellow on head and underneath and lacks brown streaking on the chest.

Stan's Notes: A common warbler in California. Flocks of hundreds are seen when northern birds join residents for the winter. Familiar call is a single robust "chip," heard mostly during migration. Sings a wonderful song in spring. Usually arrives in late September to early October. Moves quickly among trees and from the ground to trees. In the fall, the male molts to a dull color similar to the female, but he retains his yellow patches all year. Frequently called Myrtle Warbler in eastern states and Audubon's Warbler in western states. Sometimes called Butter-butt due to the yellow patch on its rump.

Look for the pink bill

female pg. 91

male

Oregon male

Dark-eyed Junco
Junco hyemalis

Size: 5½" (14 cm)

Male: A plump, dark-eyed bird with a slate-gray-to-charcoal chest, head and back. White belly. Pink bill. White outer tail feathers appear like a white V in flight.

Female: round bird with brown plumage

Juvenile: similar to female, with streaking on the breast and head

Nest: cup; female and male build; 2 broods per year

Eggs: 3–5; white with reddish-brown markings

When Seen: year-round

Food: seeds, insects; visits ground and seed feeders

Compare: Rarely confused with any other bird. Look for the pink bill and small flocks feeding under feeders to identify the male Dark-eyed Junco.

Stan's Notes: Northern birds join resident birds during winter, swelling the population. Migrates from Canada and northern parts of Minnesota to areas farther south. Adheres to a rigid social hierarchy, with dominant birds chasing the less dominant birds. Look for the white outer tail feathers flashing in flight. Often seen in small flocks on the ground, where it uses its feet to simultaneously "double-scratch" to expose seeds and insects. Eats many weed seeds. Nests in a wide variety of wooded habitats. Several junco species have now been combined into one, simply called Dark-eyed Junco (see lower inset).

Look for the black line through the eyes

Mountain Chickadee

Poecile gambeli

Size: 5½" (14 cm)

Male: A gray bird overall with a black cap, chin and line through the eyes. White eyebrows.

Female: same as male

Juvenile: similar to adult

Nest: cavity, old woodpecker hole or excavates its own; female and male build; 1–2 broods per year

Eggs: 5–8; white without markings

When Seen: year-round

Food: seeds, insects; visits seed and suet feeders

Compare: Larger than the Bushtit (pg. 129) which lacks the black cap and white on the face. Smaller than the Oak Titmouse (pg. 143), which also has a crest. Larger than the Verdin (pg. 133), which has a yellow head.

Stan's Notes: An abundant bird in the state, but more common in coniferous forests and mountainous regions of California. Prefers old-growth spruce, fir and pine forests. Feeds heavily on coniferous seeds and insects. Flocks with other birds during winter. Moves to lower elevations in winter, returning to high elevations for nesting. Excavates a nest cavity or uses an old woodpecker hole. Will use a nest box. Occasionally uses the same nest site year after year. Lines its nest with moss, hair and feathers. Female will not leave her nest if disturbed, but will hiss and flutter wings.

*Look for the
short crest*

Oak Titmouse

Baeolophus inornatus

Size: 6" (15 cm)

Male: Overall gray with brown tinges. Short crest. Small gray bill. Dark eyes.

Female: same as male

Juvenile: similar to adult, with a shorter crest

Nest: cavity; female and male line the cavity; 1–2 broods per year

Eggs: 3–6; pale white without markings

When Seen: year-round

Food: insects, seeds, fruit; comes to seed feeders

Compare: Larger than the Bushtit (pg. 129), which lacks a crest. Larger than Mountain Chickadee (pg. 141), which has a black cap, chin, and line through its eyes.

Stan's Notes: Until recently, the Oak Titmouse and the Juniper Titmouse (not shown) were considered one species: the Plain Titmouse. The Oak Titmouse is seen only in California. The Juniper is found in many Southwestern states. Seen in dry, open oak woodlands, hence its common name. Often heard before seen. A loud repeated whistle, "teewee-teeweeteewee." A very active species and an acrobat, sometimes hanging upside down from tree limbs, searching for insects. Constructs nest of moss, feathers and fur inside an old woodpecker hole or a nest box, when available. Will use a roosting box at night for protection against the cold and predators. Pairs usually stay together through the year. Often seen in mixed flocks of birds during winter. Male feeds the female in spring to reestablish the pair bond.

*Look for the
tawny belly
and undertail*

Say's Phoebe
Sayornis saya

Size: 7½" (19 cm)

Male: Overall dark gray, darkest on head, tail and wings. Belly and undertail tawny. Black bill.

Female: same as male

Juvenile: similar to adult, but browner overall with 2 tawny wing bars and a yellow lower bill

Nest: cup; female builds; 1–2 broods per year

Eggs: 3–6; pale white with brown markings

When Seen: year-round

Food: insects, berries

Compare: Say's Phoebe is similar in size and shape to the Black Phoebe (pg. 57), but it has a rusty belly and lacks the Black Phoebe's black head and chest.

Stan's Notes: Widespread throughout California below elevations of 9,000 feet (2,750 m). Nests in cliff crevices, abandoned buildings, bridges and other vertical structures. Frequently uses the same nest several times in a season, returning the following year to that same nest. Has a nearly all-insect diet. Flies out from a perch to grab an aerial insect and returns to the same perch (hawking). Also hunts insects on the ground, hovering and dropping down to catch them. Phoebes are classified as New World Flycatchers and aren't related to Old World Flycatchers. Named after Thomas Say, who is said to have first recorded this bird in Colorado. The genus, species and first part of its common name refer to Mr. Say. Common name "Phoebe" is likely an imitation of the bird's call.

Look for the deep red eyes

female

male
pg. 43

Phainopepla

Phainopepla nitens

Size: 8" (20 cm)

Female: Slim, long, mostly gray bird with a ragged crest and deep red eyes. Whitish wing bars.

Male: slim, long, glossy black bird with a ragged crest and deep red eyes, wing patches near tips of wings are white, obvious in flight

Juvenile: similar to female

Nest: cup; female and male construct; 1–2 broods per year

Eggs: 2–4; gray with brown markings

When Seen: year-round

Food: fruit (usually mistletoe), insects; will come to water elements or water drips in yards

Compare: Similar to Clark's Nutcracker (pg. 157), but the Phainopepla has a crest.

Stan's Notes: Seen in desert scrub with water and mistletoe nearby. Gives a low, liquid "kweer" song, but will also mimic other species. In winter individuals defend food supply such as a single tree with abundant mistletoe berries. Probably responsible for the dispersal of mistletoe plants far and wide. Male will fly up to a height of 300 feet (90 m), circling and zigzagging to court female. Builds nest of twigs and plant fibers and binds it with spider webs in the crotch of a mistletoe cluster. Lines nest with hair or soft plant fibers. May be the only species to nest in two regions in the same nest season. Nests in dry desert habitat in early spring. When it gets hot, moves to a higher area with an abundant water supply to nest again.

Look for the
short ear tufts

gray morph

brown morph

Western Screech-Owl
Megascops kennicottii

Size: 8–9" (22 cm); up to 1¾' wingspan

Male: A small, overall gray owl with bright yellow eyes. Two short ear tufts. A short tail. Some birds are brownish.

Female: same as male

Juvenile: similar to adult of the same morph, lacks ear tufts

Nest: cavity; uses old woodpecker hole; 1 brood per year

Eggs: 2–6; white without markings

When Seen: year-round

Food: insects, small mammals, birds

Compare: Western Screech-Owl is hard to confuse with its considerably larger cousin, the Great Horned Owl (pg. 121).

Stan's Notes: The most common small owl throughout California. An owl of suburban woodlands and backyards. Requires trees that are at least a foot in diameter for nesting and roosting, so it usually is found in towns or in trees that have been preserved. A secondary cavity nester, which means it nests in tree cavities created by other birds. Usually not found in elevations above 4,000 feet (1,200 m). Densities in lower areas are about 1 bird per square mile (2–3 birds per sq. km). Most screech-owls are gray; some are brown.

male

Look for the
rusty-red breast

female

American Robin

Turdus migratorius

Size: 9–11" (23–28 cm)

Male: Familiar gray bird with a dark rust-red breast and a nearly black head and tail. White chin with black streaks. White eye-ring.

Female: similar to male, with a duller rust-red breast and gray head

Juvenile: similar to female, with a speckled breast and brown back

Nest: cup; female builds with help from the male; 2–3 broods per year

Eggs: 4–7; pale blue without markings

When Seen: year-round

Food: insects, fruit, berries, earthworms

Compare: Familiar bird to all. To differentiate the male from the female, compare the nearly black head and rust-red chest of the male with the gray head and duller chest of the female.

Stan's Notes: Can be heard singing all night in spring. City robins sing louder than country robins in order to hear each other over traffic and noise. A robin isn't listening for worms when it turns its head to one side. It is focusing its sight out of one eye to look for dirt moving, which is caused by worms moving. Territorial, often fighting its reflection in a window.

Look for the white wing patches

displaying

Northern Mockingbird

Mimus polyglottos

Size: 10" (25 cm)

Male: Silvery-gray head and back with a light-gray breast and belly. White wing patches, seen in flight or during display. Tail mostly black with white outer tail feathers. Black bill.

Female: same as male

Juvenile: dull gray with a heavily streaked breast and a gray bill

Nest: cup; female and male construct; 2 broods per year, sometimes more

Eggs: 3–5; blue green with brown markings

When Seen: year-round

Food: insects, fruit

Compare: Look for the Mockingbird to spread its wings, flash its white wing patches and wag its tail from side to side.

Stan's Notes: A very animated bird. Performs an elaborate mating dance. Facing each other with heads and tails erect, pairs will run toward each other, flashing their white wing patches, and then retreat to cover nearby. Thought to flash the wing patches to scare up insects when hunting. Sits for long periods on top of shrubs. Imitates other birds (vocal mimicry); hence the common name. Young males often sing at night. Often unafraid of people, allowing for close observation.

Look for plume on the forehead

male

female

California Quail

Callipepla californica

Size: 10" (25 cm)

Male: Plump gray quail with black face and chin. Prominent teardrop-shaped plume on the forehead. "Scaled" appearance on the belly, light brown to white. Pale brown forehead.

Female: similar to male, lacks a black face and chin

Juvenile: similar to female

Nest: ground; female builds; 1 brood per year

Eggs: 12–16; white with brown markings

When Seen: year-round

Food: seeds, leaves, insects; visits ground feeders

Compare: Look for plume on the forehead of both male and female to help identify the California Quail.

Stan's Notes: Prefers open fields, agricultural areas and sagebrush. Not found in dense forests or high elevations. Rarely flies, preferring to run away. Roosts in trees or dense shrubs at night, not on the ground. Usually seen in groups (coveys) of up to 100 individuals during winter, breaking up into small family units for breeding. Young stay with the family group until autumn. Has expanded its range in California over the past 50 years.

Look for the small white patches on the wings

Clark's Nutcracker

Nucifraga columbiana

Size: 12" (30 cm)

Male: Gray with black wings and a narrow black band down the center of tail. Small white patches on long wings, seen in flight. Has a relatively short tail with a white undertail.

Female: same as male

Juvenile: same as adult

Nest: cup; female and male build; 1 brood a year

Eggs: 2–5; pale green with brown markings

When Seen: year-round

Food: seeds, insects, berries, eggs, mammals

Compare: The Steller's Jay (pg. 79) is dark blue with a black crest. Female Phainopepla (pg. 147) has a crest and lacks a white undertail. Look for the Clark Nutcracker's white wing patches to identify it.

Stan's Notes: A high country bird found in coniferous forests in parts of California. It has a varied diet, but relies heavily on piñon seeds, frequently caching large amounts to consume later or feed to young. Has a large pouch in its throat (sublingual pouch), which it uses to transport seeds. Studies show the birds can carry up to 100 seeds at a time. Nests early in the year, often while snow still covers the ground, relying on stored foods. A "Lewis and Clark" bird, first recorded by William Clark in 1805 in Idaho.

*Look for
the gleaming,
iridescent patches*

Rock Pigeon
Columba livia

Size: 13" (33 cm)

Male: No set color pattern. Shades of gray-to-white with patches of gleaming, iridescent green and blue. Often has a light rump patch.

Female: same as male

Juvenile: same as adult

Nest: platform; female builds; 3–4 broods per year

Eggs: 1–2; white without markings

When Seen: year-round

Food: seeds, fruit; visits ground and seed feeders

Compare: Mourning Dove (pg. 117) is smaller, light brown and lacks the variety of color combinations of the Rock Pigeon.

Stan's Notes: Also known as Domestic Pigeon. Formerly known as Rock Dove. Introduced to North America from Europe by the early settlers. Most common around cities and barnyards, where it scratches for seeds. One of the few birds with a wide variety of colors, produced by years of selective breeding while in captivity. Parents feed the young a regurgitated liquid known as crop-milk for the first few days of life. One of the few birds that can drink without tilting its head back. Nests under bridges or on buildings, balconies, barns and sheds. Was once thought to be a nuisance in cities and was poisoned. Now, many cities have Peregrine Falcons feeding on Rock Pigeons, which keeps their numbers in check.

soaring

juvenile

Look for
the banded,
rounded tip
of the tail

Cooper's Hawk
Accipiter cooperii

Size: 14–20" (36–51 cm); up to 3' wingspan

Male: Medium-sized hawk with short wings and a long, rounded tail with several black bands. Slate-gray back, rusty breast, dark wing tips. Gray bill with a bright yellow spot at the base. Dark red eyes.

Female: similar to male, only larger

Juvenile: brown back, brown streaking on the breast, bright yellow eyes

Nest: platform; male and female construct; 1 brood per year

Eggs: 2–4; greenish with brown markings

When Seen: year-round

Food: small birds, mammals

Compare: Look for the banded, rounded tail to help identify the Cooper's Hawk.

Stan's Notes: Found in many habitats, from woodlands to parks and backyards. Stubby wings help it to navigate around trees while it chases small birds. Will ambush prey, flying into heavy brush or even running on the ground in pursuit. Comes to feeders, hunting for birds. Flies with long glides followed by a few quick flaps. Calls a loud, clear "cack-cack-cack-cack." The young have gray eyes that turn bright yellow at 1 year and turn dark red later, after 3–5 years.

Look for the purple pointed mustache

male

female

Costa's Hummingbird

Calypte costae

Size: 3½" (9 cm)

Male: Green back and nape, white belly and light green flanks. Dark crown, chin, throat and down the neck, like a handlebar mustache. In direct sunlight, dark area around head reflects iridescent purple. White eyebrows.

Female: same as male, without dark marks on head, has white marks around eyes, gray cheeks

Juvenile: similar to female

Nest: cup; female builds; 1 brood per year

Eggs: 2; white without markings

When Seen: year-round

Food: small insects, flower nectar; visits feeders

Compare: Smaller size and shorter tail than most other hummers in California. Look for the male's purple cap and mustache marks on throat. Identify the female Costa's by its gray cheeks and white markings around each eye. Wings extend just beyond tip of tail when perched.

Stan's Notes: Good lighting is needed to see the green iridescence. Actively defends itself and is very territorial. Often perches, guarding territory and food supply. Gives a limited song, "tink-tink-tink," as it chases other hummers. Male performs an elaborate diving flight display to attract a mate. After mating, the female moves to her own territory to build nest and raise young.

male

*Look for
the violet blue throat*

female

Black-chinned Hummingbird

Archilochus alexandri

Size: 3¾" (9.5 cm)

Male: Tiny iridescent green bird with black throat patch (gorget) that reflects violet blue in sunlight. Black chin. White chest and belly.

Female: same as male, but lacking the throat patch and black chin, has white flanks

Juvenile: similar to female

Nest: cup; female builds; 1–2 broods per year

Eggs: 1–3; white without markings

When Seen: summer

Food: nectar, insects; will come to nectar feeders

Compare: Larger than Costa's (pg. 163), but lacking the handlebar mustache gorget (throat patch). The male Black-chinned Hummingbird often appears to have an all-black head.

Stan's Notes: One of several hummingbird species in California. Able to fly backward, but doesn't sing. Will chatter or buzz to communicate. Wings create a humming noise, flapping nearly 80 times per second. Weighing 2–3 grams, it takes about five average-sized hummingbirds to equal the weight of one chickadee. Males return first at the end of April. Male performs a spectacular pendulum-like flight over a perched female. After mating, the female builds a nest, using spider webs to glue nest materials together, and raises young without mate's help. More than one clutch per year not uncommon.

Look for the deep rose red head

male

female

Anna's Hummingbird

Calypte anna

Size: 4" (10 cm)

Male: Iridescent green body with dark head, chin and neck. In direct sunlight, the dark head shines a deep rose red. Breast and belly are dull gray. White eye-ring.

Female: similar to male, but head reflects only a few red flecks instead of a complete rose red

Juvenile: similar to female

Nest: cup; female builds; 2–3 broods per year

Eggs: 1–3; white without markings

When Seen: year-round

Food: nectar, insects; will come to nectar feeders

Compare: Anna's is similar to other hummers, but the male has a completely dark head and a white eye-ring. Female has a few red flecks on the throat. Tail extends well beyond wing tips when perched.

Stan's Notes: Common western hummingbird found from Baja, California, to British Columbia. Unknown in California before the late 1950s, it has since expanded northward and is now considered common. An early nester. Female builds a tiny nest on chaparral-covered hillsides and in canyons. Feathers on head are black until seen in direct sun. Reflected sunlight turns the male's head bright rosy red. Apparently consumes more insects than other species of hummingbirds. Generally non-migratory; some may migrate.

*Look for
the white throat
with black stripes*

Green-tailed Towhee

Pipilo chlorurus

Size: 7¼" (18.5 cm)

Male: A unique yellowish-green back, wings and tail. Dark-gray chest and face. Bright-white throat with black stripes. Rusty-red crown.

Female: same as male

Juvenile: olive-green with heavy streaking on breast and belly, lacks crown and throat markings of adult

Nest: cup; female and male construct; 1–2 broods per year

Eggs: 3–5; white with brown markings

When Seen: summer

Food: insects, seeds, fruit

Compare: Green-tailed's unusual color, short wings, long tail and large bill make it easy to identify.

Stan's Notes: Found on shrubby hillsides and sagebrush mountain slopes up to 7,000 feet (2,150 m). Like other towhees, searches for insects and seeds, taking a little jump forward while kicking backward with both feet. Known to scurry away from trouble, jumping to ground without opening its wings and running across the ground.

Look for the orange-red throat patch

male

female

Rufous Hummingbird

Selasphorus rufus

Size: 3¾" (9.5 cm)

Male: Tiny burnt-orange bird with a black throat patch (gorget) that reflects orange-red in sunlight. White chest. Green-to-tan flanks.

Female: same as male, but lacking the throat patch

Juvenile: similar to female

Nest: cup; female builds; 1–2 broods per year

Eggs: 1–3; white without markings

When Seen: spring and fall migration; winter in southern California

Food: nectar, insects; will come to nectar feeders

Compare: Identify it by the unique orange-red (rufous) color.

Stan's Notes: One of the smallest birds in California. This is a bold, hardy hummer. Frequently seen well out of its normal range in the western U.S., showing up along the East Coast. Visits hummingbird feeders in your yard during migration. Does not sing, but it will chatter or buzz to communicate. Weighing just 2–3 grams, it takes about five average-sized hummingbirds to equal the weight of one chickadee. The heart beats up to an incredible 1,260 times per minute. Male performs a spectacular pendulum-like flight over the perched female. After mating, the female will fly off to build a nest and raise young, without any help from her mate. Constructs a soft, flexible nest that expands to accommodate the growing young.

Look for the black head

male

female
pg. 109

Black-headed Grosbeak

Pheucticus melanocephalus

Size: 8" (20 cm)

Male: Stocky bird with burnt-orange chest, neck and rump. Black head, tail and wings. Irregularly shaped white wing patches. Large bill, with upper bill darker than lower.

Female: appears like an overgrown sparrow, overall brown with a lighter breast and belly, large two-toned bill, prominent white eyebrows, yellow wing linings, as seen in flight

Juvenile: similar to adult of the same sex

Nest: cup; female builds; 1 brood per year

Eggs: 3–4; pale green or bluish, brown markings

When Seen: summer

Food: seeds, insects, fruit; comes to seed feeders

Compare: The male Bullock's Oriole (pg. 175) has more white on wings than the male Black-headed. Look for Black-headed's large bicolored bill.

Stan's Notes: A cosmopolitan bird that nests in a wide variety of habitats. Both the male and female sing and will aggressively defend the nest against intruders. Song is very similar to American Robin's, (pg. 151)making it hard to tell them apart by song. Populations increasing in California and across the U.S.

*Look for
the black eye-line*

male

female
pg. 183

Bullock's Oriole
Icterus bullockii

Size: 8" (20 cm)

Male: Bright-orange-and-black bird. Black crown, eye line, nape, chin, back and wings with a bold white patch on wings.

Female: dull yellow overall, pale-white belly, white wing bars on gray-to-black wings

Juvenile: similar to female

Nest: pendulous; female and male build; 1 brood per year

Eggs: 4–6; pale white to gray, brown markings

When Seen: summer

Food: insects, berries, nectar; visits nectar feeders

Compare: Male Black-headed Grosbeak (pg. 173) is also orange and black, but it has a black head and a large, stout bill. Look for Bullock's black crown and a thin black line running through each eye.

Stan's Notes: So closely related to Baltimore Orioles of the eastern U.S., at one time both were considered a single species. Interbreeds with Baltimores where their ranges overlap. Most common in the state where cottonwood trees grow along rivers and other wetlands. Also found at edges of clearings, in city parks, on farms and along irrigation ditches. Hanging sock-like nest is constructed of plant fibers such as inner bark of junipers and willows. Will incorporate yarn and thread into its nest if offered at the time of nest building.

Look for the reddish face and the brown cap

male

female
pg. 85

yellow
male

House Finch
Haemorhous mexicanus

Size: 5" (13 cm)

Male: Small finch with a red-to-orange face, throat, chest and rump. Brown cap. Brown marking behind eyes. White belly with brown streaks. Brown wings with white streaks.

Female: brown with a heavily streaked white chest

Juvenile: similar to female

Nest: cup, occasionally in a cavity, female builds; 2 broods per year

Eggs: 4–5; pale blue, lightly marked

When Seen: year-round

Food: seeds, fruit, leaf buds; visits seed feeders and feeders that offer grape jelly

Compare: Look for the brown cap and streaked belly to help identify the male House Finch.

Stan's Notes: Can be a common bird at your feeders. A very social bird, visiting feeders in small flocks. Likes to nest in hanging flower baskets. Male sings a loud, cheerful warbling song. Native to parts of California and the western U.S., it was introduced to Long Island, New York in the 1940s, and it is now found throughout the country. Suffers from a disease that causes the eyes to crust, resulting in blindness and death. Rarely, some males are yellow (see inset), perhaps due to poor diet.

Look for the greenish back

male

female

Lesser Goldfinch
Spinus psaltria

Size: 4½" (11 cm)

Male: Striking bright yellow beneath from chin to base of tail. Black head, tail and wings. White patches on wings. Greenish back.

Female: dull yellow underneath, lacks a black head and back

Juvenile: same as female

Nest: cup; female builds; 1–2 broods per year

Eggs: 4–5; pale blue without markings

When Seen: year-round

Food: seeds, insects; will come to seed feeders

Compare: The male American Goldfinch (pg. 181) is slightly larger and has a yellow back, unlike the greenish back of male Lesser Goldfinch.

Stan's Notes: The western males have greenish backs, while males in the eastern range (Texas) have entirely black heads and backs. Some females are extremely pale. Prefers forest edges or places with short trees and a consistent water source. Unlike many other birds, its diet is about 96 percent seed, even during peak insect season. Will come to seed feeders. Late summer nesters. Male feeds the incubating female by regurgitating partially digested seeds. Pairs stay together all winter. Winter flocks can number in the hundreds.

Look for the black forehead

male

winter male

female

American Goldfinch
Spinus tristis

Size: 5" (13 cm)

Male: Bright canary-yellow finch with a black forehead and tail. Black wings with white wing bars. White rump. No markings on the chest. Winter male is similar to the female.

Female: dull olive-yellow plumage with brown wings; lacks a black forehead

Juvenile: same as female

Nest: cup; female builds; 1 brood per year

Eggs: 4–6; pale blue without markings

When Seen: year-round

Food: seeds, insects; comes to seed feeders

Compare: The male Lesser Goldfinch (pg. 179) has a greenish back. Pine Siskin (pg. 83) has a streaked chest and belly and yellow wing bars. The female House Finch (pg. 85) has a heavily streaked chest.

Stan's Notes: A common backyard resident. Most often found in open fields, scrubby areas and woodlands. Enjoys Nyjer seed in feeders. Breeds in late summer. Lines its nest with the silky down from wild thistle. Almost always in small flocks. Twitters while it flies. Flight is roller coaster-like. Moves around to find adequate food during winter. Often called Wild Canary due to the male's canary-colored plumage. Male sings a pleasant, high-pitched song.

Look for the dull yellow head and chest

female

male
pg. 175

Bullock's Oriole

Icterus bullockii

Size: 8" (20 cm)

Female: Dull-yellow head and chest. Gray-to-black wings with white wing bars. A pale-white belly. Gray back, as seen in flight.

Male: bright-orange-and-black bird with a bold white patch on wings

Juvenile: similar to female

Nest: pendulous; female and male build; 1 brood per year

Eggs: 4–6; pale white to gray, brown markings

When Seen: summer

Food: insects, berries, nectar; visits nectar feeders

Compare: Female Lesser Goldfinch (pg. 179) is half the size of female Bullock's Oriole and is dull yellow underneath, unlike female Bullock's pale-white belly.

Stan's Notes: So closely related to Baltimore Orioles of the eastern U.S., at one time both were considered a single species. Interbreeds with Baltimores where their ranges overlap. Most common in the state where cottonwood trees grow along rivers and other wetlands. Also found at edges of clearings, in city parks, on farms and along irrigation ditches. Hanging sock-like nest is constructed of plant fibers such as inner bark of junipers and willows. Will incorporate yarn and thread into its nest if offered at the time of nest building.

Birding on the Internet

Birding online is a great way to discover additional information and learn more about birds. These websites will assist you in your pursuit of birds. Web addresses sometimes change a bit, so if one no longer works, just enter the name of the group into a search engine to track down the new address.

Author Stan Tekiela's homepage
naturesmart.com

American Birding Association
aba.org

The Cornell Lab of Ornithology
birds.cornell.edu

eBird
ebird.org

Christmas Bird Count
www.audubon.org/conservation/science/christmas-bird-count

Great Backyard Bird Count
gbbc.birdcount.org

Feather Atlas
www.fws.gov/lab/featheratlas

Zooniverse
www.zooniverse.org
(several citizen science projects pertaining to birds)

Checklist/Index by Species

Use the boxes to check the birds you've seen.

Glossary

birdsong: A series of musical notes that a bird strings together in a pleasing melody. Also called a song.

brood: A family of related bird siblings that hatched at around the same time.

brood parasites: Birds that don't nest, incubate or raise families, such as Brown-headed Cowbirds (pp. 39 and 105). See *host*.

call: A nonmusical sound, often a single note, that is repeated.

carrion: A dead and often rotting animal's body, or carcass, that is an important food for many other animals, including birds.

citizen science: Science projects that harness data from the observations of everyday people; the Christmas Backyard Bird Count and the Great Backyard Bird Count are examples.

colony: A group of birds nesting together in the same area. The size of a colony can range from two pairs to hundreds of birds.

coniferous: A tree or shrub that has evergreen, needle-like leaves and that produces cones.

cover: A dense area of trees or shrubs where birds nest or hide.

crop-milk: A liquid that pigeons and doves regurgitate (spit up) to feed their young.

deciduous: A tree or shrub that sheds its leaves every year.

display: An attention-getting behavior of birds to impress and attract a mate, or to draw predators away from the nest. A display may include dramatic movements in flight or on the ground.

dimorphic: Bird species in which the males and females look different (the Red-winged Blackbird, pp. 45 and 111, is an example)

excavate: To dig or carefully remove wood or dirt, creating a cavity, hole or tunnel.

fledge: The process of developing flight feathers and leaving the nest.

flock: A group of the same bird species or a gathering of mixed species of birds. Flocks range from a pair of birds to upwards of 10,000 individuals.

habitat: The natural home or environment of a bird.

hatchlings: Baby birds that have recently emerged from their eggs. See *nestlings*.

hood: The markings on the head of a bird, resembling a hood.

horns: A tuft or collection of feathers, usually on top of a bird's head, resembling horns.

host: A bird species that takes care of the eggs and babies of other bird species. See *brood parasites*.

incubation: The process of sitting on bird eggs in the nest to keep them warm until they hatch.

iridescent: A luminous, or bright, quality of feathers, with colors seeming to change when viewed from different angles.

irruptive migrator: A bird that migrates irregularly and suddenly.

juvenile: A bird that isn't an adult yet.

lore: The area on each side of a bird's face between the eye and the base of the bill.

migrate: The regular, predictable pattern of seasonal movement by some birds from one region to another, especially to escape winter.

molt: The process of dropping old, worn-out feathers and replacing them with new feathers, usually only one feather at a time.

morph: A bird with a color variation. Morphs also sometimes occur in mammals, reptiles, amphibians and insects.

mute: The inability to make or produce audible sounds.

necklace: The markings around the neck of a bird, as seen in the Killdeer (pg. 113).

nape: The back of a bird's neck.

nectar: A sugar and water solution found in plant flowers.

nestlings: Young birds that have not yet left the nest. See *hatchlings*.

plumage: The collective set of feathers on a bird at any given time.

prey: Any critter that is hunted and killed by another for food.

raptor: A flesh-eating bird of prey that hunts and kills for food. Hawks, eagles, ospreys, falcons, owls and vultures are raptors. See *prey*.

regurgitate: The process of bringing swallowed food up again to the mouth to feed young birds.

sublingual: Under the tongue; some bird species have anatomical adaptations that allow them to carry seeds or food under their tongue.

suet: Animal fat, usually beef, that has been heated and made into cakes to feed birds.

thermal: A column of warm air moving upwards; some birds use them when soaring.

trill: A fluttering or repeated series of similar-sounding musical notes given by some birds.

twitter: A high-pitched call of a bird. See *call*.

undulating: In an up-and-down motion, usually referring to a bird's flight pattern.

Embrace Nature with

BIRDS

- Birds of California
- Birds of Prey of the West

PLAYING CARDS

- Birds of the Northwest
- Birds of the Southwest
- Mammals of the Northwest
- Mammals of the Southwest
- Trees of the Northwest
- Trees of the Southwest
- Wildflowers of the Northwest
- Hummingbirds
- Loons
- Owls
- Raptors

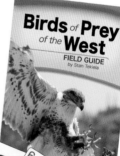

More from Stan Tekiela

CHILDREN'S BOOKS

Baby Bear Discovers the World
Critter Litter Southwest
The Cutest Critter
Do Beavers Need Blankets?
Hidden Critters
Jump, Little Wood Ducks
Some Babies Are Wild
Super Animal Powers
What Eats That?
Whose Baby Butt?
Whose Butt?
Whose Track is That?

WILDLIFE APPRECIATION

Backyard Birds
Bird Migration
Wild Birds

POPULAR BIRD BOOKS

Birds of the Northwest
Birds of the Southwest
Bird Trivia

About the Author

Naturalist, wildlife photographer and writer Stan Tekiela is the originator of the popular state-specific field guide series that includes dozens of titles, including *Birds of California* and many other guides to birds and birding in the West. Stan has authored more than 190 educational books, including field guides, quick guides, nature books, children's books and more, presenting many species of animals and plants.

With a Bachelor of Science degree in natural history from the University of Minnesota and as an active professional naturalist for more than 30 years, Stan studies and photographs wildlife throughout the United States and Canada. He has received national and regional awards for his books and photographs and is also a well-known columnist and radio personality. His syndicated column appears in more than 25 newspapers, and his wildlife programs are broadcast on a number of Midwest radio stations. You can follow Stan on Facebook and Twitter or contact him via his website, naturesmart.com.